E. H.
A M
CHRISTIAN
MYSTIC

New Dawn books by Hugh Black

Reflections on the Baptism in the Holy Spirit
Reflections on the Gifts of the Spirit
Reflections on a Song of Love (1 Cor 13)
A Trumpet Call to Women
The Clash of Tongues: With Glimpses of Revival
Consider Him (Twelve Qualities of Christ)
Battle for the Body
The Incomparable Christ
Gospel Vignettes
Reflections from Abraham
Reflections from Moses: With the Testimony of Dan McVicar
Christ the Deliverer
Christian Fundamentals
Reflections from David
Pioneers of the Spiritual Way
Revival: Including the Prophetic Vision of Jean Darnall
Revival: Personal Encounters
Revival: Living in the Realities

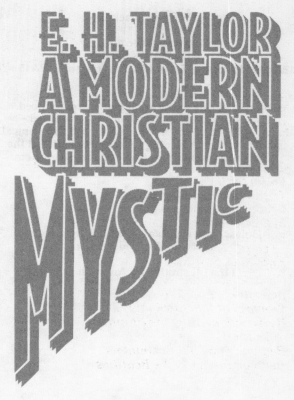

E. H. TAYLOR A MODERN CHRISTIAN MYSTIC

compiled by

Hugh B. Black

NEW DAWN BOOKS
GREENOCK, SCOTLAND

First published 1994 by
NEW DAWN BOOKS
10A Jamaica Street, Greenock, Renfrewshire, PA15 1YB

ISBN 1 870944 18 6

Unless otherwise stated, biblical references
are to the Revised Version.

Line illustration by Anne Thomas

Production and Printing in England for
NEW DAWN BOOKS
10A Jamaica Street, Greenock, Renfrewshire, PA15 1YB by
Nuprint Ltd, Station Road, Harpenden, Herts AL5 4SE.

This book is dedicated to Pauline Anderson, without whose vision and drive it was unlikely ever to have seen the light of day, and to a group of people who gave Miss Taylor much practical help in her closing years when she suffered much from the aftermath of a stroke — Grace Gault and Betty Logan, her first 'nurses', Alison and Mary Black, Grace Gilchrist, Sen., Ruth Gollan, Jennifer Jack and Irene Morrison.

Acknowledgements

The compiler wishes to express his gratitude to his wife Isobel and daughter Alison, and to Pauline Anderson, Jennifer Jack, Eckbert Kruger and Stuart McCorkindale, for a variety of helpful contributions to the production of this book. Particular acknowledgement is made to those who have kindly allowed their written or spoken word to be included: Ivy Anslow, Mary Black, Grace Gault and Sheila Robertson.

Contents

Spiritual Conflict and Testing

Premonitions of Eternity

Vision of a Work

Foreword

In our earliest days as children, we learn much of the world around us: an accumulation of knowledge based upon our experience. As we take our first weak and faltering steps we begin to learn the principles of balance; the correction of a parent warns us of the danger of fire or of water. Unrestrained, we may touch a cooker or a fire and learn, sadly this time through painful experience, some of the dangers of our environment. We grow to adulthood with a knowledge of our surroundings, with a capability of surviving in a sometimes hostile world; learning our limits, our confines, and knowing the restrictions of our human body, we take care to avoid, as far as possible, injury and hurt, pain and suffering. We as human beings set boundaries around our lives, sometimes consciously, often unconsciously, and live within these walls for our own safety and protection, knowing that to cross them will bring risk and danger to ourselves.

In the new birth in Christ we enter a new world, a spiritual world — often with enthusiasm and excitement and with great ambition to make much of this wholly new life, different in kind and in experience from anything we have known before. Sadly, many fail. To a great extent our Christian lives fall short of early goals and have little impact upon the non-Christian world around us. Whether through our own poor understanding of the immeasurable heights to which a life in Christ can rise, or by the company in our earliest Christian days of those who never expected much out of spiritual life anyway, and teach such, we enter this new life, tragically, stillborn; or, at most, as chicks which have hatched from the shell but never spread their wings — missing, therefore, the whole purpose of existence. This, unfortunately, is the way of too many Christian lives: applying limits, confines and restrictions where they were never meant to be, lowering expectations until our spiritual lives are in greater part nominal and certainly without power, placing God within the same walls that border our natural lives.

The lady about whom this book is written and whose teaching is included here was not like this at all. Under the ministry of Miss Elizabeth Taylor, through her preaching, teaching, conversation or letters, one became aware of God — an awesome, holy God, unapproachable except in Christ; a God distinct in His three Persons; a God of fire, light, purity, power, and yet a Father loving His lost creation and sending His beloved Son to find His children and bring them home. Miss Taylor lived in and taught of the spiritual dimension, leading many through to a depth in spiritual experience and revelation of God unimaginable. The confines and restrictions one had subconsciously placed around the Christian life vanished like insubstantial shadows, as the sunrise of revelation of a limitless God broke upon a gathered congregation and we were given the knowledge that this Supreme Being, this awesome and holy God, desired to make His home in our hearts and lives. Truly Emmanuel, God with us.

I am delighted to see this book released, that those who were not able to be under her ministry directly, or who are the spiritual children (or grandchildren!) of lives to whom God appointed her to minister, may also benefit from the depth and quality of spiritual food which she faithfully imparted to her God-given 'bairns' whom she loved and who deeply loved her.

Alone with Thee, amid the mystic shadows,
　The solemn hush of nature newly-born;

Alone with Thee in breathless adoration,
In the calm dew and freshness of the morn.

Mr Hugh Black, the author of this book, and Miss Elizabeth Taylor worked together in a spiritual partnership for the greater part of half a century. I am very grateful to him, knowing her as he did, for gathering these nuggets of spiritual gold together that many lives hungry and thirsty for the deep things of God may feed richly in these pages and grow strong in their Christian lives, breathing the air of that heavenly land while yet on earth.

Bishopton, Renfrewshire   *Paul J. Sharkey*

Introduction

Elizabeth H. Taylor (1909–1991) was a woman greatly used of God in the Struthers Movement, of which she could be regarded as the main founder.

She was a real 'mother in Israel' and was spiritually greatly gifted.

Over the years she taught holiness and sanctification consistently and deeply. Spiritual gifts operated through her very markedly — particularly interpretation, prophecy, faith, knowledge and discernment. She was much used in bringing people into the baptism in the Holy Spirit and, in her later days, in the ministry of deliverance.

From the opening of Struthers Memorial Church in 1954 Miss Taylor and I shared the ministry. In 1983 she suffered from a stroke which greatly incapacitated her, and for some years before her death in 1991 she was unable to continue preaching.

Her testimony as recorded in my book *A Trumpet Call to Women* (New Dawn Books, 1988) raised much interest outwith her own circles. In her own church where she was so highly regarded it was greatly welcomed. Thus there has been considerable anticipation for the publication of this present book.

The book falls into four parts. Part One, based on personal conversations, gives some indication of Miss Taylor's insights into spiritual life, and a wide variety of themes is opened up.

Part Two gives a very illuminating insight into Miss Taylor's dealings with one of her spiritual daughters. A deep experience of the latter and Miss Taylor's involvement in it are of interest and value.

Part Three contains one of Miss Taylor's sermons, 'The Lost Horizon'. This has been much used as it has been widely distributed in tape form and gives a taste of what Miss Taylor's preaching was like.

Part Four, 'Home Call', takes us to her death and funeral.

The way in which the first part of the book came into being was indicated in an appendix to my *Gospel Vignettes* (New Dawn Books, 1989). I quote:

After publishing Miss Taylor's testimony in *A Trumpet Call to Women*, I became aware that some of the things she said had roused great interest. One lady who had long profited from Miss Taylor's ministry was far from satisfied with the amount of detail I had elicited and really put pressure on me. 'I am sure', she said, 'there is much more gold there which could be mined. And', she continued, 'you'll regret it if you don't get it all out.' I, however, felt that my writing where Miss Taylor was concerned was done with the publication of the book and I had no intention whatever of acceding to the request. She kept on at me, however, and then a strange thing happened. It occurred to me that maybe I really *should* do this. The feeling grew until it became a conviction and I found God was in it. I think that basically I am not a very suggestible person, if I may put it that way. I stoutly resisted writing books at all for a long time despite pressure from others, including Miss Taylor, until I became convinced God wanted it. In writing I have met Him very deeply and know as deep anointing in this as in preaching. Similarly, I have found God deeply present when I visit Miss Taylor and go 'mining for gold'. As many readers know, she suffered from the effects of a stroke, and again and again I arrive to find her suffering from angina attacks. Frequently a skin condition causes her great irritation, and an ulcerated leg has caused her to be house-bound. Sometimes she looks grey with illness, but as I gradually turn her mind to the deep things of God, she becomes animated and the ills of the flesh seem to fall off. There comes the glow of God and I find that my notes can scarcely keep up with her flow.

The friend who put such pressure on me was Pauline Anderson. In a footnote accompanying the above, I explained in more detail the circumstances in which she persuaded me to 'dig for gold':

> The lady felt that it would be tragic if Miss Taylor should die and take with her to the grave a depth of experience and spiritual knowledge which could be so valuable to others. She had been quite persistent on this theme several times before, pointing out how I might, indeed how I would, she was sure, deeply regret my negligence when it was too late! I had not been at all co-operative or encouraging. I really had no intention of doing anything about it at all! On this occasion, however, a strange thing did happen. As my friend was speaking, I became aware that something was happening to her even as she spoke. I sensed that she was receiving revelation from God right on the spot. There came over her an absolute conviction that this thing was to be done, that it was not merely a notion of her own — but that it was in fact the will of God. She was quite obviously deeply affected and I could not remain unmoved. She told me later that her spirit had been burdened over this matter for quite a time and that she really had no peace until I agreed to do as she suggested. I began for the first time to consider the matter positively and I must admit that conviction came over me too. I was almost surprised to hear myself say, somewhat sheepishly and maybe more than a trifle reluctantly, 'All right, I'll do it.'

The material in Part One was gathered in conversation over a period of a few years, and its present style and arrangement reflect the informal nature of its origin. Some order has been imposed: the material has been sifted and divided into sixty-two sections, each with a numbered heading. These have been organized in a sequence corresponding in general to the main themes with which they deal: the growth of a spiritual creature and the development of gifts and ministries; spiritual conflict and testing; premonitions of eternity; the vision of a work of God. The reader will, however, find that these are overlapping themes. The wise reader will discover not only food for the mind but nourishment for the spirit, as it is impregnated by something of the atmosphere which the author inhabited.

Miss Taylor's words in Part One are preserved not absolutely verbatim, but as close to it as was possible in the form of notes written on the occasion. Those who have heard her speak on spiritual subjects will recognize her voice sounding throughout these pages. Editorial comments and significant insertions appear in square brackets or in the notes. My own conversational contributions and occasional 'diary' entries are italicized, to distinguish them from Miss Taylor's words.

Finally, it has usually seemed desirable to preserve anonymity by substituting a letter of the alphabet for personal names mentioned in Parts One and Two. Beginning with the letter A— , alphabetical order is strictly adhered to. An individual appearing more than once will generally be designated by a different letter on each appearance.

I

INSIGHTS INTO SPIRITUAL LIFE

Becoming Spiritual Creatures

1 *PRAYING INTO A VOID — OR FOCUSING ON CHRIST*

In prayer so many people pray into a void, not to a Person but to an unknown place — hopefully and sometimes not so hopefully, as though not speaking to God. In real, effective prayer we have to be where we focus on Christ; we are not left with an unknown void. He gave us a form extremely familiar: we come to God through Christ. The focus is on a Person. Christ is God the Son. When we focus on Christ, we focus on God.[1] This affects the quality of prayer. People who are in this place emanate God. Because of their contact with Him God emanates through them and He fills the atmosphere. People praying to a void are like sounding cymbals. The person who has learned to speak to God in prayer finds a love, an interchange of love, which is shed out to the congregation so that there is no sounding brass or tinkling cymbals. Everything is wrapped up in love for God and in the love of God.

Note

[1] Note that prayer is to the Father. We come through Christ to the Father.

2 PRAYER

For me prayer is nothing other than speaking with God
as a friend speaks with a friend. One thing that came to
me over a period of illness was about the king of Israel
who was told by the prophet to strike the ground with
an arrow (2 Ki 13:18). He was foolish only to strike it a
few times. Had he done it often he would have had
more victories. People are inclined to ask for things and
leave off too quickly. They don't pursue the matter. The
story of the one who came seeking bread at midnight
and kept on asking, points the same lesson (Lu 11:5–8).
Eventually the other got up and gave the bread. There
follows the injunction to pray. Persistence in prayer is
required. Sometimes He keeps you waiting until you
are desperate. Then there comes the witness that you
are heard, and when He has heard we have the witness
that we will get what we have asked for. But there is not
necessarily anything spectacular about it.

A burden of prayer is something God gives. You
cannot give it to yourself. A burden was laid on me to
get into prayer for two young men to the point where
God had heard me.[1] I then waited for what God would
say. It is not a one-sided matter. It is something
between two entities — the human and the divine. I
don't expect an answer unless I have touched that point
of deep awareness that God has heard me and
responded. When that happens I do expect the thing
prayed for to be accomplished. For me it is not a case of
storming the gates of heaven; but in a quiet waiting
before Him I have found the ear of God. There comes a
great confidence that having been heard, the petition
shall be granted. There is great weight on the word,
'When He, the Spirit, is come, He will lead you into all
truth.' To me this is more than any ministry: to be
where the Spirit Himself can teach the truth as it is in
Christ Jesus — the truth about many things. It covers the
whole spectrum of both the life and the death of Christ,

for example the hidden days of Easter. It is stupendous to have the Spirit teach us.

When one starts out to pray one must have a right attitude to God: reverence, deepest worship, holy fear. One is approaching the Almighty. There is no brash rushing in: 'Give me this or that.' It is as Christ taught us: 'Our Father, hallowed be Thy name.' This expresses a deep attitude arising from the inner man; it is spiritual — not a mental exercise. There is the supreme knowledge that no earthly person's prayer in itself is worth the breath it costs. Its value is that it is offered in the name of Jesus — just as, with a cheque, a bank honours the name of the signatory. As Peter put it, healing was in Christ's name (Acts 3:6). The name of Jesus brings the answer, not the vehemence of the suppliant. When we get a true experience and knowledge of that fact it transforms prayer from a hopeful 'perhaps' to a confidence that God will honour.

Prayer is a relationship with God, like getting to know a person, what they approve and disapprove. The knowledge is instinctive, and so it is with God. Prayer — the quality of prayer — is an outcome of a relationship. The spiritual being (the part born of the Spirit) desires nothing but to be in communion with God, by prayer, with conversation. There is no formality about it; it is instinctive and spontaneous — otherwise it is not prayer, but a mere intellectual exercise. You find yourself in intercession for somebody, holding them up in the presence of God, often without knowing when it started.

Note

[1] These two were deeply backslidden. There was no indication that they would come back to God when God brought them in spirit before Miss Taylor. He promised that they would be restored and they both were, very remarkably.

3 CARRYING THE PRESENCE

There is a sense in which God clothes Himself with a person — as with the late Principal Jeffreys. This man could come into a hall and it was like a door opening as the presence of God came rushing in. He was, as it were, an embodiment of that presence. People felt at ease and covered. There is a cover, though not according to the extreme 'shepherding' idea: it is not the person that is the cover, but the presence they carry. When people went into the Town Hall in Greenock during Mr Jeffreys' campaign in 1929, they sensed they were covered by God, although they did not necessarily recognize what was happening. You lost all nerves and uncertainty. There are those like this now — of whom you [HB] are one. I have heard it said of myself, but one is not conscious of it in oneself — otherwise it might be ruined.

One becomes a vehicle, a carrier of the presence of God which covers a whole company. It operates inside and outside of meetings and can reach out to cover individuals. In your case it was more difficult for me to give you this cover if you were far away: I couldn't always locate you. My spirit locates a person more easily if I know where they are. If they are outwith my geographic knowledge something is lost. When you go (as you did, for example, yesterday), I like to know where you are going and how you are going. My spirit goes out and finds you. There is a positive standing in before God on your behalf. It is not something I can do myself; this is true shepherding. It irks me when people speak of needing a cover, meaning a human cover. Such people have a slight smattering of truth, a blurred vision of it.

Satan perverts things — he takes something beautiful and distorts it. He takes a truth and twists it. God floods a place through a human, and foolish people think it is the human who is the covering. The covering comes through such a one, and it is of course true that if that person was not there, it would not be there, for they are appointed for that purpose. I think every child of God should be in that place to carry that anointing. We disciplined our lives and became not only carriers but transmitters.

4 THE EMANATION OF GOD

— Two people are seemingly equal. One prays, and it is good, but it does little for the company. Before two sentences of the other are spoken, God is pervading the atmosphere. Why?

It comes from union with Christ — the condition of the relationship of our spirit with the Holy Spirit. If people have found the inner place of communion they slip into a union with God and the Holy Spirit speaks through them. They are so tuned to Him that He can do that.

— How does one move from one position to the other?

By a lifelong discipline: living in the Spirit continuously, not just at crisis moments — experiencing a deep, abiding fellowship. Some people only find communion with God when they want something. Others live in that place and seldom have to ask for anything. 'Your heavenly Father knoweth ye have need of all these things.'

— What is the relationship between that communion and the gifts? In my view, when that relationship is maintained, God flows through the gifts of the Spirit.

Yes, the gifts come into operation powerfully and with effect. Being in that relationship with God brings prophecy, for example, into effectiveness. Preaching becomes the living word, and people can see and feel as well as hear.

— How do you explain the degree of the emanation of God which came through George Jeffreys, for example?

His relationship with God: 'If ye abide in me...' He lived that way — in Christ. It is like someone living in a room full of fragrance: the fragrance attaches itself to a person. So does an ugly odour. I think he abode in that relationship continuously.[1]

Note

[1] The story is told of a valley of roses in Roumania whose scent was so strong that it lingered all day on those who had been there. See Mrs Charles Cowman, *Streams in the Desert* vol. 2 (Marshall Pickering, 1966; © 1966 Cowman Publications, Inc.), reading for 10 November.

5 SALVATION

My first revelation of Christ was at conversion when under the awful light of God there was intense conviction. I was cut off from God with a sense of uncleanness: yet I was very clean, no smutty company, no going to cinema... I was particularly clean, yet at that hour abhorred myself. I was filthy and terrified. In these moments when I was aware of separation from God through my unclean condition, it was as though I was looking down into hell — a vortex of darkness and pain in which there was no hope of an end, a sense of incompletion and being cut off from God. Into that awful situation came a gentle shimmer of pure incandescent light — in between the terrible light of the holiness of God and my uncleanness. In *that* light things not considered sin were shown as God saw them; it was quite different from the human estimate of good and evil. It was rather a judgment on what possessed the mind which was hidden and secret. The gentle, shimmering light — a form which was glowing with this — was kind. I came into a dimension that had no fear; I sensed that in this One there was deliverance. I lifted my being to Him. At that moment I did not know who He was. I appealed to Him and discovered that He was my Saviour.

With a look of ineffable love in His eyes He touched and healed and cleansed me, and all I could say was, 'I'm clean, I'm clean.' I had been filthy in the eyes of God. The peerless perfection of Christ had shown it up in a way that I couldn't bear. In His eyes there was forgiveness, no accusation. And (something few seem fully to realize in their own lives) I was born of the Spirit, reborn with a capacity to embrace spiritual things as they are. We can exercise this capacity if we will, and if we don't allow the old 'born of the flesh' nature to block off the flow of spiritual life — spiritual affections, spiritual affinity with God through Christ.

6 *THE NEW BIRTH*

The new birth is terribly misunderstood and under-valued. In our natural birth we live after and for the things of the flesh. So with our new birth we ought to live after and for the things of the Spirit. These things clarify as life goes on and we live in God through Christ. A vital part of the new birth is the entering of a new life. Old things are done away and a different way of life begins. How watered down the teaching of the new birth has become through the centuries!

7 LACK OF DESIRE

— Why do some evidence little desire for the spiritual depths?

I really think its roots are in what happens to a person at conversion. How deep does it go? Was there merely mental assent, or did the person become a new creature? The old nature has no desire for spiritual things. There is far more involved in the simple act of conversion than people realize. The natural is born of flesh of the will of man, with desires of the human race predominant. The other is born of the Spirit into the likeness of Christ, with Christ's desire. We become new creatures if we are truly born again. One can at times measure something of the depth of the new birth experience by the quality of the life that is lived afterwards — its desires and functioning.

8 BECOMING SPIRITUAL CREATURES

God's intention even when we are in our bodies is to make us spiritual creatures, not bound by the confines of human imagery. I am confident that in that moment when we are changed we become spiritual creatures and we begin to know as we are known.

Many people think that when we read of old things passing away this refers merely to old habits and so forth, when really it refers to old faulty perception, for example of the truth as it is in Christ. We enter a new dimension altogether, seeing not as in a glass darkly but face to face.

9 *KNOWING CHRIST*

If we would take time to meditate on the word of God,
we would not make so many mistakes. For example,
what it means to be born of the flesh, and what it means
to be born of the Spirit. So few meditate deeply on the
truth as it is in Christ. When I was baptized in the Spirit
I wasn't in any great measure attracted to certain ministries — they were perfect and to be desired, but the
driving force in my life was to know the truth as it is in
Christ.

I ultimately lost interest, in a sense, in books that
described Christ. I wanted the truth concerning Himself from Himself. That scripture becomes true: 'He that
hath seen Me hath seen the Father.' Being in Christ
means being in God. You are enfolded in the bundle of
life. It is as if God is in the van and Christ walks with
you and the Spirit seals the rear — you are encased and
enclosed in that Trinity. You learn to walk and to talk
with Christ in that relationship. He wants to speak of
the Father and then you hear the Father speaking of His
Son — of how He loves Him and of His perfection and
what He requires for Him from the saved sinner: first
and foremost an all-compelling love until Christ
eclipses everything and everyone else in life, until you
find the intrinsic value of Christ Himself. It is a revelation, something only God can give, and only to those
who become spiritual creatures through applying their
thought life to spiritual matters. The full knowing of
Christ comes by revelation, not by an action of the
mind. It can only be given to those who are spiritually
tuned. When born of the flesh we spontaneously attend
to things of the body — its well-being, food, hygiene —
full care of the body. This should be transferred when
born of the Spirit. Our full occupation then is transferred from caring for and attending to the natural, to
caring for the spiritual creature. The same attention
should be given: feed, cleanse, care for it, guard it.

If anything goes wrong with the body we attend to it: do the same immediately with the spiritual life.

10   KNOWING THE FATHER

One thing Christ endeavours to do with great persistence is to lead us to the Father. He has one overwhelming desire — that we may know the Father. He meant it when He said, 'I am the Way,' meaning He is God and the Way to God. 'He that hath seen me hath seen the Father.' It is almost painful when we feel the impact of His desire that we should know the Father — it is one of the things He died for. He draws people, not to Himself, but to the Father through Himself. He died to do that; there is an utter selflessness about it. He wants praise to go to the Father.

Of me He said, 'I bring you one who loves You.' I had been converted into a lover of God and was fully repentant. I will never forget the earlier moment when God revealed Himself to me — that He existed and was right where I was. I was face to face with Him, and there was a sternness. He was displeased, very displeased with me because of my denying His existence. Christ stood between us, between me and that wrath — that stupefying wrath. He came between and took it instead of me. It was my sin, my deliberate sin. I had known very well there was a God. In bravado I had taken up the stance I had taken, and He made me pay for it. I had been brought up in a godly home and had been in contact with God as a child, and was without excuse.

11 *A TOTAL GIVING OF ONESELF TO CHRIST*

— How does one give oneself completely to Christ? Surface issues may be given, indeed inner issues committed, but the awareness comes from time to time that there is a world beyond — a yet deeper level, a place where, though earth life continues, the life is possessed by heaven: a condition where God's breath moves freely and completely unhindered through a vessel. Where is the key?

The key is separation unto God and unquestioning obedience. One following this path will be asked to do much against his own ideas and desires that will be inexplicable in many cases. He is not just to resign himself to these situations, but to accept with very sweet pleasure: 'If this is the way, I am taking it.' No heroics, no melodrama, but almost a monstrous experience in the sense of continuous self denial. Again and again the rational self will cry out, 'God wouldn't ask me for this!' It will rebel, and feel it. It is not our natural way to say, 'All right, Lord, so be it'; but in acceptance there is peace. This goes on to the end of life and becomes a very acceptable way. A scripture has been living for me for a fortnight past: 'In Him we live and move and have our being.' Our moment-by-moment experience is God-consciousness. We live in obedience to God. There is no move or change in life without the knowledge that God has changed it, and we can do literally nothing without Him. It is almost like water baptism. You become immersed in God. He is bearing you up. He shall separate the holy from the 'holy':[1] it comes to a very fine line of demarcation in life. There is unremitting discipline for twenty-four hours a day. Even sleeping, you are disciplined. It is a way of life. Think of an athlete preparing for a race: everything goes, evenings are spent in preparation, days in preparation. All his thoughts are geared towards it. Few want the discipline that goes with the ambition. Is he prepared to give over the thought life as well as his actual practical life until the thing is accomplished? To achieve his end he has to maintain this state of separation from himself.

When my body has been in fearful pain and discomfort, I have remembered the occasion of the cattle pulling the ark (1 Sam 6:14). At the end they were sacrificed: that was their reward. I remember standing in Terrace Road [in Greenock] and giving my life to God as a blank cheque: I wouldn't complain about anything He did or allowed. Now it is all right if I have to endure what I do. I meant my bargain and so did He. People forget that God hears them when they make vows. God means what He says and He expects us to mean what we say.

Note

[1] The Bible speaks of separating the holy from the unholy. Miss Taylor seems to be indicating that for the life separated to God even the 'holy' (i.e. things not normally regarded as unholy) may not be what is holy for that individual. In a somewhat similar fashion we sometimes say that 'the good is the enemy of the best'.

12   *SEVERED UNTO GOD*

There is a state of being severed unto God: a giving of the life to God, absolutely severed from other things. 'I will sever thee.' This is different from the normal idea of separation or sanctification.

[It carries with it the thought that that which is severed can never be put together again. It is irreversible, as is the type of union with God which accompanies it.][1]

Note

[1] The reader is reminded that square brackets denote the compiler's insertions.

13 *HEALING*

I was lying quietly thinking on Christ, silent worship going up from my heart.[1] I don't always speak these things out. It is rich, spontaneous worship of spirit. He stood beside the bed and said, 'Would you take healing now were I to give it to you?'

'Yes, if it is Your will, Lord.'[2] I saw in Him the divine Healer and the quality of healing. He Himself was perfect; He had no need of healing. Again there was that touch of His fingers on the top of my head, and His life passed through me — a life vibrant with strength and vigour. I arose immediately and prepared some food, got ready, and went out to my work — forty years' migraine gone. The lingering fragrance of His personality and of His love remained through the whole day. He had come and offered the healing. It was as when somebody gives you a gift not because it's a special day, or a celebration, but simply because they love you.

Notes

[1] The occasion was one when Miss Taylor had had to go home after a Sunday evening service with a blinding attack of migraine. For many years she had suffered greatly from ill health, particularly from migraines. She frequently felt sick but was unable to be sick. At times she was very near death's door.

[2] I remember when this happened being deeply impressed with Miss Taylor's attitude to healing. When it was offered she did not immediately grasp at it as I imagine most people would have done. She wished to have only what God wanted.

14 *GIFTS*

[On being questioned about gifts of the Spirit, Miss Taylor said that at first she did not know what to ask for.]

I was not wise enough. I asked God to give as pleased Him — but promised that I would use all He did give when He wanted. There were no arguments. I have no time for people who say, 'Is it me or God?' They can know perfectly well if they wish.

The healing of a young man was the first challenge to the promise that I would do what He told me [sec. 15]. It was the same with my first deliverance.[1] I had never seen a deliverance. I was told to go — and I went. It was the same with regard to all of the gifts He might give. It is so vitally important that having promised to do the thing, we do it. There may be nobody else who knows of our promise — but God knows.

Note

[1] This, I think, refers to the deliverance of a young man who later became one of our church leaders. Not long after his conversion he came to one of our early meetings in Balvonie Conference Centre in Scotland. At the very beginning of a service a demon manifested itself and he fell to the floor screaming. Miss Taylor went to him immediately and signed to me to do likewise. There came a powerful anointing and a sense of victory through the congregation. I have often thought that that demon had no chance. It came screaming out.

We both went on to be used in deliverance — she very powerfully, and I at first more intermittently. In my case there came a later point when I was thrust forcefully into this field.

15 *A CONTINUOUS STATE OF READINESS*

When given some of the gifts, especially prophecy and interpretation, I realized I was representing God speaking to His people. My life had to be under a very, very severe discipline — every day of life — so that when God spoke there would be no admixture. The voice was to be like a trumpet He Himself had tuned. There should be no need to have hurried, immediate cleansing. We should live in a clean state to be used, so close to God that there is no mistaking His touch — no question, 'Is it me? Is it God?' It should be just the same as when He spoke to Ananias about Paul: Ananias was ready to go. God is the same yesterday, today and for ever. He expects us to live in that place. As, for example, when He once told me to take you [HB] and A — to visit a sick person: we were *all* to be in prime condition for the work that was to be done.[1] When Christ becomes your life you live in that place. You become like Him. He was always ready. Some of the selflessness of Christ and His devotion to the Father comes to the person who lives and walks with Christ consciously — in a definite, positive way.

Note

[1] My recollection of this occasion is still fairly clear, although it happened over forty years ago, before our own church was formed. Miss Taylor asked a local church elder and myself to accompany her to visit a very sick young man. It later transpired that God had instructed her to pray for the lad. This was breaking new ground for her and she really tried to shelter behind the two of us. We both prayed, I fancy rather ineffectually. God then put pressure on her and she obeyed. The boy was healed.

16   *INNERNESS OF REVELATION*

Revelation does not come by a mental process. There is a gift of discernment — discernment of spirit (it can mean the discerning of the spirit of a person as well as of evil spirits). Again it involves an amalgam of gifts, including, for example, the gift of knowledge.[1] You meet a total stranger and speak for a moment. It is as if something is thrown on a screen, not from you but to you. There is revelation of that person's spiritual being and potential — of their spirit, whether a good one or a bad one. It is almost a character reading, because you get a knowledge of their natural inner being as well as of their spiritual being. All parts of your being are deeply immersed in the Spirit. The Bible speaks of living and walking in the Spirit (Gal 5:25). This means a very prescribed life that very few Christians are willing to live.

I recall the severity of the discipline of life God brought me into, not just of acts, but of mind. There was no allowance for untoward levity of thought, or self-seeking (seeking something good for oneself) — there just was not to be a self. It meant every moment of every day was to be lived in the conscious presence of God for His approval. His disapproval was devastating if I wandered from the known path. This approach applied to every day of every week of every month. If in any company a certain kind of lightness arose I was not allowed to enter in; I had to be different from people generally, totally different in attitudes and opinions and decisions, so that it showed and others knew it. Normal people hate this. You lose the herd instinct completely; you become an individual before God. This can affect your style of speaking, your style of dressing, your style of approach to other people. It means you take quite a lot of abuse and do not retaliate. All of life is disciplined so that God can give revelation because you are under His discipline. It seems very severe, and is very severe — no doubt about it — but when you are living in that place God can reflect on that calm life without distortion. I suppose the natural ability to judge is put into abeyance. Often spiritual revelation is quite different. You have got to be prepared to accept that and forego your own natural impressions. You can come into a place where you meet a person and know whether God's hand is on the person for His own purposes — but only if you are living in that place and your own life is in total abeyance.

Note

[1] For further information see Hugh Black, *Reflections on the Gifts of the Spirit* (New Dawn Books, 1988).

17   *EARLY SEPARATION*

In my very early days, a youth group were having a
singsong, with choruses, etc. They were making an
evening of it with special dress — a kind of watered-
down party. I went happily enough to it with others (I
was playing the piano), and in the midst of it came
under conviction: I was not to be involved with them in
it. I was to be different. Convicted, I rose from the piano
and stopped. They were astonished; nobody else could
play. You have got to be prepared to be different — to
separate the holy from the 'holy' (sec. 11). You have got
to know what is permissible and what is not — not by
human standards but by direction of the Spirit. You
come in for a lot of criticism that is often foolish and
silly. You are judged as being uppish, 'better than other
folk'. Living obviously to standards others are not prepared for, you become a reproach. They get rid of their
sense of guilt if they get rid of you. Extremism is one of
the things you will be charged with. You have got to be
prepared to go it alone. You are not allowed to have an
over-intimate friendship at a human level — although
you may have friends.

18 SPIRITUAL PERCEPTION: THE KNOWING OF THE UNKNOWN

The knowing of the unknown, like so much else that is spiritual, does not come at the bidding of the mind but is related to a way of life. What happens then is like being at an airport when luggage is coming along on the carousel: as your own luggage approaches, you recognize it. You live in a realm where there is continuous communion with God the Spirit. An occasion arises when something of interest relating to someone occurs to you, like their baggage coming along: you recognize it as theirs. It is not, as with a suitcase, recognition with the natural mind, but it is recognition of something you never saw them with; it is an instinctive knowing, or rather revelation; it is not found by reasoning. You recognize it as pertaining to them.

How do you know someone's character or personality in this way? It is tied up with one's own relationship with the Spirit, and is not just received in flashes but is ongoing, all the time. He can transmit knowledge He has when there is quietness in an unbroken relationship with Himself. There is a place of tranquillity, where nothing can distort the revelation. There can be silence almost tangible, spent in contact with the Holy Spirit — not when one is particularly seeking, but experienced as a way of life.

A person comes before you. People have facades and you see right through these. The Spirit takes down that screen and you see into the mind and heart and spirit and being. The last one this happened with was B — . In the natural realm she is brusque and abrasive. I saw past that: inside there is a kindness, a kind of mothering — not only of her own children but of people generally. Part of her yearns to comfort and bring others into a place of peace and tranquillity. The knowledge of this kind of thing is something that comes in the course of communion of spirit with the Holy Spirit. He brings the person before you and gives revelation. You don't ask about so-and-so and so-and-so. You have no notion of who it will be who will come before you. It happened with C — . She covered herself well — put up an opaque facade. I saw past to her inner being, to a strength and spiritual quality that could be completely overlooked — an unwavering, steadfast spirit.

It was like the occasion when I first saw you [HB]. I saw the back of your head and shoulders; I had not seen your face; we were in a church building and hadn't spoken. There came a knowledge that God had put His hand on your life in a very particular way. Such revelation stems from a particular relationship with the Holy Spirit. There is a transmission of thought, of purpose. You don't ask. He gives, and when He does, it is very clear, crystal clear.

As with the relation between purity and power, there is a tranquillity which is the doorway to revelation. You must have purity to have power. You need tranquillity where secrets are transmitted, with no fleshly knowledge to prevent this. God instructed me to be totally apart from a gossipy relationship with people. My mind was not to be filled with natural facts which would have distorted revelation. Thus when God spoke through me to individuals, they knew it and knew I had no knowledge of the situation of which I spoke. This brought the knowledge that it was God sharply to them.

19 BRINGING OTHERS INTO THE REVELATION OF CHRIST

This ministry is one about which little is known.[1] This kind of revelation of Christ is a distinct experience.

— *What happened when a person was brought to you?*

An action of the Spirit. No human power is of any avail in this realm. As Christ said of the Spirit, 'He when He is come will guide you into all truth.' (He also said: 'I am the truth.' To be led into truth is to be led into Christ.) 'He will take of the things that are Mine and reveal them unto you.' He reveals Christ. He makes Christ a person — not a vague, nebulous name. Christ baptizes in the Spirit and now the Spirit reveals Christ outwith the mind. This has nothing to do with human thought. He comes as a divine, supernatural Being. The spirit of the disciple is tuned to a different level, appreciation, awareness of Christ — not to a Babe in the Manger. He meets the Son of God. 'Unto us a child is born, unto us a Son is given' — a Son not born, but eternal. Human faculties cannot apprehend this, so an operation has to be carried out on the human spirit. This results in a union between the spirit and God. He puts a right spirit within us. A person is given a start in a different spiritual realm, totally unknown previously — a realm of relationship with the Godhead.

No life is complete without coming into this place. Some come into it in their own aloneness with God, others through ministry. Christ actually becomes formed within a person. The gift or ministry of bringing others to this place is very rare. The person concerned has to dwell very deeply in God before he (or she) can be used to bring others in. From such lives there comes an emanation of Christ. Sometimes when they pray or speak in public His presence pervades the atmosphere. (Mr George Jeffreys, the founder of Elim, was one such. He carried an aura of God with him.) If you work all day in a perfume factory you carry fragrance; if you work in a cowshed you carry the smell that goes with it.

This inner place is not one which you visit from time to time, but one in which you live. If you dwell there you carry the atmosphere in which you dwell. In God you live and move and have your being. You become saturated in God. Thus His fragrance flows out. In Him your mind (spiritual mind) dwells.

In ordinary life two people may at first be casual friends. They may later become close friends and their lives may be joined. They then know each other in a different way. So with the soul and God. In this relationship, there is an accurate knowledge of the will of God. When He speaks the soul knows. When you are in a positive relationship with Christ you know His voice. 'My sheep know My voice.' This is a realm of certainty.

Much revolves round living and moving and having our being in God. Few live there. You can't have this with a casual relationship. There is no jumping around. You are rooted and grounded in Christ.

Note

[1] This section originally appeared in the appendix to *Gospel Vignettes*, in connection with a testimony in that book.

20 *ON APPENDIX TO* GOSPEL VIGNETTES

[To one who wrote to her she recommended that part of *Gospel Vignettes* dealing with the ministry of the revelation of Christ. Those seeking a deep relationship with God would find it described there. Commenting on the book when it first appeared, she said with regard to her own contribution that she was pleasantly surprised, and added the following.]

I hadn't thought it possible to transmit certain spiritual things in words. A certain quality of spirituality is not easily reduced to human language. It is as when you ask a person to give testimony to the baptism in the Spirit: it is not really in the realm of human expression.

— I think you have good reason to be pleased.

I am very pleased. I read it as though somebody else had composed it; I dissociated it from myself. I am very pleased at the quality of it.

21   MISCELLANEOUS

The spirit of the prophet is subject to the prophet (1 Cor 14:32). This is not to be confused with the operation of the Holy Spirit. When the human spirit runs riot it brings disrepute on the gifts. I have no disagreement with your teaching in *The Clash of Tongues* — it is pretty much what I would have said myself.[1]

What is that funny name you have given that other book — the French word — *Gospel Vignettes*?

— How do you like it?

Oh, I like it, but think it will be a bit of a hurdle for most folks to pronounce. It's breaking out of the familiar mould, anyway. It's original.

Note

[1] Hugh B. Black, *The Clash of Tongues: With Glimpses of Revival* (New Dawn Books, 1988). The reference is presumably to chap. 14, pp. 100–4.

22 BLIND FAITH

A common feature runs through spiritual life. In the first instance you must take a step in blind faith (as with salvation). You accept it, unknowing, when He is opening up a new line — as with healing, deliverance, etc. No pattern is revealed: you go in blindly and do as you are told. Satan may say, 'You'll look a fool,' but you must have confidence that the thing will be as God has planned. I remember my first laying of hands on others for the baptism. I didn't know what would happen, but there was an assurance on my spirit that God would do it. So with deliverance. And so with prophecy: in this case maybe just a sentence or two given before speaking; very occasionally, the first part of the message.

So in our relationship with God we come in out of the cold — as with D — at the moment: there is a dawning consciousness that there is something there, a coming into something — being awakened to the knowledge that there is something one doesn't have but could have. Then the question arises as to how to get it. The fact that God has spoken is enough: it is the same thing as an accomplished fact. This has to be accepted. When I fell on Tuesday night I said, 'Lord, it's just You and me.' I believed He would uphold me and I did as I would have done if someone had been lifting me. I had to act in faith.

How do we come into a place of total dependency on God for living? I learned in that night what it is to have total dependency on God. I had to walk; my head was spinning; there was a total, practical, real leaning on God for His upholding till I got to a place of safety. You take what God says without any physical evidence. That is a secret of a relationship with God. He has said, and it is sufficient. 'I will uphold you.' 'Uphold': on Tuesday night it was so vital that I wouldn't fall on my way to the bedroom. It is a very practical relationship, not airy-fairy, up in the sky. It means an unquestioning accepting of His word. 'I will keep thy feet from falling': suddenly the scripture is a blazing, glorious truth, revealed as the word of God in a working sense. But I had to take the actual step — to walk before I felt the upholding. As in the baptism: we have got to give our vocal chords, we have got to act consciously in a practical sense. So many won't become practical: it's all going to be a spiritual exercise in which they have no responsibility — and so they don't get the baptism. In ministries there has got to be practical application without the evidence of the senses. There comes a very warm sense of having entered into a unity with the Trinity.

Spiritual Conflict and Testing

23 *PRIDE OF THE DEVIL*

You lose pride when you become a spiritual creature. Pride and envy put Satan out of Heaven. When you get a sniff of the envy of Satan against Christ it could make you afraid: there is such a force of envy.

[Miss Taylor commented that she thought a recent attack from Satan was directly connected with the taking of these notes. She has thought of him as Lucifer, son of the morning, beautiful 'beyond compare', but full of rottenness.]

24 *SATANIC STRATEGY REVEALED*

[HB'S DIARY: *Last night I had a phone call from Miss Taylor. Referring to E — (an adult we both knew), she indicated she had had a vision of a spirit of uncleanness minded to affect young boys. There would be an attempt to put a spirit of uncleanness through certain young lads whom she named. The demon threatened that if she interfered she would pay dearly for it. There will be need of deliverance for the man concerned, and this is likely to be violent. The revelation in her own spirit is that the name of the evil entity is The Wolf, out to destroy that which is clean. She has been threatened. 'If there is deliverance ministry,' she said, 'none of the boys are to be anywhere near. The evil spirit will seek a place to enter and hide.' It is the first time she has ever quite seen things this way, where the evil power's future programme is revealed in such detail. Boys are the target. It is one of the most malignant, vicious spirits she has ever come on, reminding her of the one that struck her immediately prior to her stroke. This present one is determined not to be cast into the void. The man concerned must go through deliverance before he works with boys. The revelation involved for her a horrible experience. She was threatened with dire consequences if she moved in any way to thwart the plan. Since she decided to contact me, there has been a cloud over her.*]

It was like watching a screen with a magic lantern. There was a slide put in over which I had no control, and another, showing the innerness of the person, until a whole revelation was given — stage by stage.

In some strange way the spirit seeking to destroy E — reminds me of F — 's case. It has the same kind of blackness and force, an ancestral spirit[1] associated with an old cult; you know how virulent they can be. The black art of these early generations is something frightful in its force and power — something not to be found normally in Europe today. It goes into the warp and the woof and produces bondslaves of fear. It is that type of evil that has arrayed itself around E — and would enter him if possible.

Note

[1] I.e. a spirit working through the generations — not the spirit of a deceased person.

25   *FALLING INTO THE HANDS OF GOD*

[Speaking of a certain individual Miss Taylor said, 'He will know the pangs of hell. He let Satan pour through him against God's anointed. While he was doing it he was bringing the wrath of God on his own head. It is a fearful thing to fall into the hands of God. He took the devoted thing, ripped it to shreds, derided it, scorned it. He will know the pangs of hell while on earth. Spiritually he is a broken, done man. He will know a living death while still on earth. His spirit will find no rest.'

Regarding another, she was apprehensive. While she felt there was forgiveness for him in her spirit, he found no absolution on earth but carried a load of sin into eternity with him, unrepentant.

Of another she said, 'He had better watch himself — he is on very dangerous ground. Read of the people who harmed David. "Vengeance is mine, saith the Lord. I will repay." Think of the awful deaths of Shimei and Absalom.'

Regarding another she said, 'I was sick when I saw her struck — I knew she had been fatally wounded. The person became like a shell, still sounding.']

26   CONFLICT

[HB'S DIARY: *I felt a movement of darkness over the last five to six weeks, but a lightening over about the last ten days. Miss Taylor agrees that it has been so, and that at the time it was quite virulent.*]

. . . . .

— *Any feelings of the rumblings of Satan?*

I think they have subsided to a great extent. I think he thought he was going to get another innings but discovered he wasn't.

27   HELLISH LAUGHTER OF SATAN

I still hear the hellish laughter of Satan when a person was taunting me — 'Where is the greater glory now?'[1] I wish I could put into words what took place in spiritual places over that time — the revealed purposes of God and the revealed anger of God. There were two people, both of whom despised my spiritual ideas of revelation. With a sarcastic sneer one repeated some of the things I had said — quoted them with derision in his voice.

Note

[1] This was with reference to a declared promise of God.

28   *A TRAGEDY*

[Of one about whose eternal destiny she was very unhappy:]

There was a movement in deep realms of darkness against me through him. While it is true that no man can pluck a soul out of the Father's hand, this does not mean a man cannot take himself out. I think that on one day this man sealed his destiny. Now he is a pawn: he has to do what he is told.

29 *THE ATTACK OF SATAN*

My first awareness of a particular coming of Satan was on one ordinary night, and it happened as I was going to sleep.[1] I became aware of a presence in the room, and a nameless fear came over me. I did not know what I was afraid of. Then there seemed to be a moving of the bed and bedclothes. I located the presence over beside the window, a little distance away. Gradually the presence became almost bodily, as real as though a human being was in the room. The fear was coming upon me from that direction. This continued for quite a time; I did not know what it was and let it go on. But I knew it was spiritual. It became too fearful, too horrifying to describe. Fear overwhelmed me. The evil power brought such fear that I cried out to God to come to my aid. I still did not know it was Satan, but it was he himself who was in the room. The room was filled with the chaotic sound of movement, of bodies. I can see it all again. There was a crescendo of fear such that I was terrified. I cried out that Christ would come and deliver me — come between me and the horror.

When I was on the point of breaking and of my nerve giving way, a peace came upon me and I metaphorically turned to look behind me. Christ was standing there and the evil power shrank (one might almost say) until it disappeared, crying out that it could not stand the presence of Christ — it could not remain in it, I suppose. In that moment came unquestioning knowledge of the lordship of Christ. Never again was the experience so terrifying, though repeated many times. I had learned to go into Christ. He always came, and the devil always went. Always there was the touching of the bed, the changing of its position, the shaking of it or pulling at the bedclothes so that they were drawn off me. But all this lost its power to terrify. Christ was dominant.

This continued for two or three years, until I lost my

fear of the devil — not that I became brash, but I learned that his coming and that of Christ were synonymous. So I was never driven to an extremity. Both Christ and the devil always stood in a particular position: the devil at the window and Christ at the back of the headboard: each had a clear location.

One night Satan came in when I was almost asleep. I sensed a movement at the bottom of the bed — movement of a body, as of an animal, black and furry. It came up and lay across my chest, putting its head down under my neck, so that I found myself suffocating with the pressure on my chest and throat. I tried to pull it away, but it fixed its teeth in the back of my neck. In the morning there were red marks left.[2]

— How did it depart?

The entity just faded out, like a whipped cur with its hind end down, surly. Its size was that of a small dog or a big wild cat.

Satan often made suggestions, jibing at God: did I still trust Him, when he (Satan) had access to where I was? Did I still trust the protective promises? He constantly questioned the lordship of Christ. He tried to persuade me I had been completely deceived by the Bible. Quite often the next day I found a promise in the Bible having been fulfilled.

— What do you think Satan's strategy was?

To bring me into a thraldom of fear to himself and to persuade me that Christ was not over him. His activity would continue until I sensed the sound of movement and had an awareness of evil presence — until I could say, 'It's you again,' and go to sleep, having called on Christ. These events brought into my being the undeniable knowledge of the lordship of Christ over Satan. I saw the inglorious exit of Satan on each occasion. These were wonderful experiences when fear was overcome and I came into confidence in Christ. Christ never allowed me to be a victim of the power of darkness.

— *Why did God allow this?*

To bring me into the place of unalterable confidence in the truth concerning Christ — of His supremacy.

— *Did all this come before you were used in deliverance?*

Yes.

— *And how is it related to it?*

It gave me almost a contempt for Satan and a knowledge that he had to flee before the presence of Christ. He could not remain.

All this was lying in the background when I was used in deliverance. Christ was always an orb of light — not a brilliant, hurting light, but a soft light. It was as though the beam from the face of Christ was directed right on to Satan and he couldn't bear the light. He just disintegrated and faded.

These were quite terrifying experiences for an inexperienced person. I sometimes think that the revelation of Christ at conversion had some bearing on my ability to hide in Him with confidence (sec. 5). I expected Satan to flee at the presence of Christ.

It was wonderful to realize that what began in abject terror became something of no account in the confidence of the knowledge of Christ's presence and power.

At last Satan had to acknowledge he had lost the game. There was ultimately not a tremor of fear at his presence.

After many years he came at odd moments to attack the lordship of Christ. I told him that if he killed me I would die proclaiming the lordship of Christ. He would threaten to do this if I didn't stop — and he is threatening right now to kill me if I don't stop telling you all this.

[Miss Taylor went on to speak of her grandmother, who, she thought, may have had something to do with her own fearlessness.[3]

An emanation such as came through my grandmother can sometimes be more effective than preaching.

Satan is not pleased with this now.

No wonder he hates our church — he hates our being used in deliverance. Now Satan's kingdom is being battered. It was a wonderful experience night after night to see the victory of Christ at that earlier time. In a sense this was connected with the coming ministry of deliverance.[4]

No wonder that for years there has been antagonism against the church and its members.

Notes

[1] I remember when the events described here were taking place. At first Miss Taylor said little about it but ultimately let me know what was happening. At that time I had little knowledge of these things and was much relieved when I discovered that Madame Guyon went through very similar experiences. At that time this was the only case in literature of which I knew. In her *Autobiography* (Moody Press, n.d.), Madame Guyon describes her experience as follows:

> After the accident which befell me (fall from the horse) from which I soon wonderfully recovered, the Devil began to declare himself more openly mine enemy, to break loose and become outrageous. One night, when I least thought of it, something very monstrous and frightful presented itself. It seemed a kind [of] face, which was seen by a glimmering blueish light. I don't know whether the flame itself composed that horrible face or appearance; for it was so mixed and passed by so rapidly, that I could not discern it. My soul rested in its calm situation and assurance, and it appeared no more after that manner. As I arose at midnight to pray, I heard frightful noises in my chamber and after I had lain down they were still worse. My bed often shook for a quarter of an hour at a time, and the sashes were all burst. Every morning while this continued, they were found shattered and torn, yet I felt no fear. I arose and lighted my waxcandle at a lamp which I kept in my room...I made use of my little light to look all over the room and at the sashes, at the very time the noise was strongest. As he saw that I was afraid of nothing, he left off all on a sudden, and attacked me no more in person.
>
> (pp. 243—4)

Miss Taylor told me that her experience in conflict with Satan gave her a backbone of steel and stood her in good stead when she was later used in deliverance ministry.

2 I was tempted to omit this part (it is so fearful) and I might have done so lest readers judge it as farfetched had it not been for the celebrated experience of Lester Sumrall which has become so well known. In the Philippines he was called to minister to a woman: 'Some unseen creature apparently was biting her, leaving deep teeth marks on her neck, arms and legs.' The woman in this case was a demoniac, and was completely delivered. See Peter Wagner, *Territorial Spirits: Insights on Strategic-Level Spiritual Warfare from Nineteen Christian Leaders* (Sovereign World, 1991), p. 44.

3 This was a very godly lady who greatly influenced her granddaughter. As a child, Miss Taylor often stayed with her and learned about real Christianity at first hand. She realized that Christ was intimately real to her grandmother and through her sensed the reality of His presence. This had an abiding influence on her life. For further detail see *A Trumpet Call to Women*, p. 110.

4 Norman Grubb wrote of Rees Howells, suggesting that he opened the way to a new dimension not for himself alone but for the whole church:

> Through the position gained in his intercession for the consumptive woman, God's servant had become sensitive to His voice in cases of sickness in a way that he had never been before. It had been a long spiritual climb in her case, but now he found that in a moment he could take the word of the Lord. He had so many of these cases at that time that it looked as if this would be his special ministry; and he often said from that period, that he believed a new era of healing would break forth in the Christian church. Perhaps only eternity will reveal how much the Spirit's intercession and believing through him has contributed to the revival of spiritual healing which has been witnessed in many parts of the church in recent years.

See Norman P. Grubb, *Rees Howells Intercessor* (Christian Literature Crusade, 1952), p. 95. For the story of the consumptive woman, see ibid., chap. 11.

In my view Miss Taylor broke through to a place of power, and many of us as a result have been enabled to go in and reap the fruits of victory. Evidence of this accumulates every day. For examples, see my *Christ the Deliverer* (New Dawn Books, 1991).

30   *AN EARLY ATTACK OF EVIL*

I remember while ministering to one man a blow on the chest so real as to produce a physical reaction. There was the knowledge that something had moved from him. For years I didn't think anything like this would happen to me. I had supreme confidence in God's protection — then I discovered that He wanted to know if I would trust Him when He seemed not to stand by when He put me through the fire. Was my confidence a fair-weather confidence? He wanted more than that. He wanted trust, when all my natural faculties were shouting out that He had let me down, He had betrayed me. He asks a great deal from us if He is really going to transform us.

The after-effect was congestion in my chest for a long time. The man concerned had very bad chest trouble at that time.

The spiritual consequence was that it brought me very, very close to God.

31 *ANOTHER ENCOUNTER WITH EVIL POWER*

When an evil power was being put out of a man, it lashed at me with its tail. It struck the right side of my head and left me with a headache for an hour afterwards — it was the right side of my brain that was paralysed [in the stroke a few days later]. The evil one overstepped himself, for never had I such a relationship with God as after that: I learned to live and move and have my being in God. His support has been literal. The awful experience was a means of revelation of Himself and of His love. Things Satan had earlier tried to give the lie to were all proved in indisputable ways.

In its descent the evil spirit in the form of a snake (a big serpent with a tail like the trunk of a tree) was so furious at being driven out that it lashed out at me in going. I think God allowed this. It brought a situation where I have known God as I never would in normal circumstances.

32   *LOVELY REVELATION AND UNSAVOURY INTERLUDE*

God spoke to me about B — (sec. 18). I hadn't looked for anything for her.. It came spontaneously — one of the things I liked about it was that there was no conjuring of anything up (not that I would do that). There was no doubt about whom it was for. No doubt others would like this, but it is not something I can do. B — is well favoured. It is not often that God explains why He is doing a thing. The fact that she accepted her situation without question meant an awful lot in spiritual places. I like it when God speaks to me about others. He seldom speaks to me about myself. I am often suspicious when people are exalted in their so-called visions. In the Bible, God's speaking to people is often for others and not for themselves.

The day after I arranged to have the message passed on to her about this, there was poltergeist activity. As I sat in the kitchen, an empty cake box was left on the work-top across from where I was sitting. My eye was caught by a shadow. I looked up, and there was the box circling round the light. (Each time it passed the light, it caused the shadow.) As I looked, it fell, touching my head and coming on to the ledge from which I was eating. It then fell to the floor. I was determined that it should fly no more and put my foot on it. It was a weird experience, horrible, especially coming last thing at night. It was an awfully silly thing — like the mischief a poltergeist gets up to. I associate the incident with my activity related to B —. It was an irritating thing: it could get on your nerves. It could get to a stage where you could look at things and wonder if they were moving. It was not as though I was half asleep. I had no notion of sleep at that particular moment.

33   *A DANGEROUS EPISODE*

[At 2 a.m. on Sunday 9 April, Miss Taylor heard someone at the main door of the tenement in which she
lived. There was a shout: 'Let me in, let me in!' as the
door was hammered. At 3:20 a.m. her bell began to ring
and stopped at 3:40 a.m. A man opened her letter box
and looked in; she saw two eyes. From time to time he
pressed the buzzer. Perhaps the police were after him
and he wanted to get into a house. At 8 o'clock in the
morning the police took two men away from the tenement in handcuffs — one who lived above her and
another from nearby. One had a big plastic bag with
presumably stolen goods. A boy of fifteen was charged
by the police; presumably he had been sent into houses
by the men. This boy had a very soft voice. He had tried
(if it was the same boy) to get into Miss Taylor's house,
offering to give the names of two men who had been
earlier at her door to whom she had refused entry.

Miss Taylor was remarkably unmoved, without a
tremor of fear; she couldn't understand this. She said
she was as cool as though it wasn't happening. At one
o'clock on the Tuesday morning she felt tension, but
did not let it take over. She could have got really upset
but didn't. This was probably reaction. If the men had
made any attempt to force the door she would have
phoned the police. For a time a thumb was on the bell
almost continuously.

It emerged later that a boy had mugged two old age
pensioners — a man of eighty and a woman of seventy-
nine. Both were taken to hospital. The man had a broken shoulder and a broken arm. Presumably this was
the same boy who had tried to get into Miss Taylor's
house. This boy was put on a murder charge. He had
used a stick to the old people and attempted to murder
them. He stole cigarette lighters, a rosary, a purse and
£5 cash. He was also charged with attempting to break
into the home of an 83-year old person, and was put on

breach of peace charges for offences outside two other elderly people's houses — one of which presumably was Miss Taylor's flat.]

In the afterward you can see the picture: in the midst of what seems horrendous there was peace. God proved Himself 'a very present help' in time of trouble (Ps 46:1), and the truth of the word, 'Thou wilt keep him in perfect peace, whose mind is stayed on thee' (Isa 26:3), was wonderfully demonstrated. In the mêlée I turned over in perfect comfort for a good night's sleep.

The house was not empty — I was not alone. I was aware of a personality [angelic or divine] in the house with me. That was probably why I didn't phone the police. It was as though events had not reached that degree of seriousness (although of course from another point of view the matter was far past that).

34 *PEACE IN ACCEPTANCE*

[HB'S DIARY: *Miss Taylor not well today; she can't go out. I am taking notes in her room. I actually caught a look on her face which I associate with death. I don't know that she will be long with us.*]

In my present illness Satan is hammering, hammering, hammering — he accuses God of lies.

If this is God's will for me I don't want anything else.

With acceptance there comes a warmth: you are in that place of unspeakable beauty. I once said, 'I give you my life as a blank cheque with no comeback.' He is doing what I asked Him to do — bringing a deep, deep contentment in God, a confidence and a trust.

35   *CONCERNING A SPIRITUAL DAUGHTER*

She had better be warned that if she goes on the course she has started [of following Christ fully], she is going to be in danger of the big guns.

.   .   .   .   .

— How safe is she?

She is eternally safe in the hands of God. But she must leave herself totally in God's hands. She will go through the fire. If He puts her through He will be with her in it. The fire will refine and make her increasingly sensitive. He will not put her through if she is not fit; if she could not stand it He would not put her through.

He wants to take her to a place of total dependency. She must be brave. It is an evidence of the life of Christ in the believer that they go through similar circumstances to those Christ faced. ('My God, why hast Thou forsaken me?') It is something to rejoice in if God considers you strong enough to go through the fire.

36 *TEST OF GOD'S LOVE*

We are expected to endure the fire and still be faithful, even in the seven-times heated furnace. The branch that bears fruit He prunes. He chastises the son, not the foundling. Being left with an affliction can be a mark of honour. It was so for Job. It was so for Mrs Moules who died in agony with cancer after leprosy work.[1] In the story of the kine who drew the Ark of God, they themselves were sacrifices. This indicates a depth in God that few glimpse, let alone enter. The human part starts back. 'My thoughts are not your thoughts.'

Note

[1] Mrs Moules was the founder of the Worldwide Evangelization Crusade's leprosy work in Africa.

37 *ON THE PREPARATION OF THIS BOOK*

I am being battered because Satan is coming with insinuations and is angry that these things are being put down and heaven made attractive to people. It brings Christ into the centre of attention, and Satan can't stand that. He knows that the things being written ring of spiritual eternity.

. . . . .

I myself am very pleased that these things will not go with me to the grave and be buried, if they can help somebody else.

. . . . .

[Various possible titles for the book were discussed, amongst which was 'Reflections from within the Veil', but no firm decisions were made at this point.]

38   A CAMP FAILURE

There was dreadful warfare in heaven over a particular camp. God was displeased. 'The iniquity of us all was laid on Him': I sensed that our iniquity regarding our failure over that camp was laid on Christ. The Bible speaks so literally of things. People were disregarding the word being faithfully preached to them — there was careless behaviour between meetings as though they hadn't been in the presence of God. There was a failure to appreciate the treasures poured out on them. God doesn't just go on speaking to be ignored, casting pearls before swine. Mealtimes were atrocious for the lightness, levity and noise of the company.[1]

I came home on the Saturday under terrible distress until I went to bed at night. I wakened on Sunday staggeringly conscious of Christ, with a vividness I hadn't known before. It was as though He was lashed to a pole and being scourged and the Spirit was saying, 'I have laid on Him the iniquity of the company.' I heard the words, 'Reproach hath broken My heart.' A charge of exquisite pain passed through me from head to feet. It was heartbreaking — an agony of spirit. 'A wounded spirit who can bear?' He carried away the reproach. A frightful atmosphere of unhappiness had come in — things had gone wrong somewhere — and I saw these things in spirit.

Let it be known that there is a very great reality between God and ourselves. There is not a great gulf fixed in the sense that we are over here and He is over there, and we can do what we like. I will never forget the pain that went through me — and *I* was not bearing the reproach.

[From a personal letter written to one of my daughters in the month following this incident comes a further description of the event and its sequel:]

Arriving at camp I was pleased to find a sense of having come into an atmosphere already rich with the presence of God. Then I stood to give the word and was almost visually confronted with Satan, who disputed every word. The conflict was dreadful and lasted until Monday (from Saturday). Then I got a word from God which brought full victory, and Satan was driven off. The following meetings were increasingly profitable until one in which God made Himself manifest in a breathtaking manner. I had been speaking on texts relating to the 'Cloud of His Glory' — the cloud which followed His people, rested on the tabernacle etc., the cloud into which the people were baptized (1 Cor 10:2) — and it was then that God baptized the company unto Christ in the cloud. There remained during that night and through the forenoon of the next day an awe and astonishment with increasing revelation of the Godhead; then Satan did what he had tried to do at the beginning of the week.

He found entrance through a number of less spiritual people. An unseemly levity pervaded the lunch in the dining room. I was 'told' to intervene and demand silence but I did not do it. I don't know if it would have had much effect, things had gone so far; people were by then out of the Spirit and into the natural. However that may be, God withdrew and desolation filled my being. The truth of the situation did not strike anyone else but myself until after the evening meeting. Your father and [certain others] knew something serious had happened but did not fully understand until we met...when the day was over. I communicated to them something of the enormity of the event and the truth of the matter swept over us...God was gracious and before the breaking up of camp He wrought much good in many lives — but — but — the glory had departed.

We came home and about half an hour after entering my house I collapsed under the most awesome experience I have ever had. It was that I was taken beyond the natural into the spiritual suffering of Christ on Calvary. There came upon my spirit an experience of condemnation upon sin and the outpouring of the wrath of God upon sin which was insupportable, at this same time experiencing the indescribable agony of being forsaken by God. This lasted for about a week. It was clearly made known that the condemnation and wrath were upon the sin of the people in that they had lightly esteemed the glory of God. At the same time I was caused to know that I was not guilty of that offence; nevertheless I had to bear the judgment. My health gave out, but that was incidental; the torment was spiritual. The following week there was a slight lifting of the pain but still a heavy darkness in the soul; the Bible was silent; there was no help anywhere. I was God-forsaken. I sought death — life was untenable.

A moment came on the following Monday night (I had not gone to the meeting; my soul had reached the lowest hell) when a gleam of light penetrated the darkness and on Tuesday morning I wakened to find the 'night' of torment had gone and a new 'day' filled with the joy of reunion with God had dawned.

How little we know of the suffering of Christ because of sin. The faint glimpse given to me has left a scar upon my being which will never be erased, nor do I want it to be.

The days have passed since; there has been a deep sense of the favour and blessing of God but not the full joy of complete restoration to 'that' place — you know what I mean — until Sunday night last. The choir were rehearsing when the Spirit came upon us. It was lovely; the few remaining of the congregation were caught in; then it seemed as though heaven opened and a rush of the *power* of God's glory filled the church. We could not stand (we had been standing singing when the Spirit came upon us); we had to sit down and bow our heads on the book board. For me it was not only spiritual but physical impact, and I know it was the same for many others. Surely this is an earnest of the power of the Spirit which shall come when the church is revived, power which shall cast down mankind bodily, as well as spiritually, before an holy and awesome God. Can it be that the earnest is a sign that the full flood is not too far away? God grant it may be so. Now I know the joy of the favour of God restored and have come again into 'that' place.

Note

[1] 'Atrocious' was Miss Taylor's judgment from a deeply spiritual point of view. The company's behaviour would not have been so regarded by many less spiritual people.

Premonitions of Eternity

39 *A TASTE OF HEAVEN*

A fleeting visit to eternity — where as usual in quietness I felt the Spirit coming on me. An astonishingly bright light came down and enveloped me. My awareness was of moving out of time and into eternity as a sinless soul — the condition one goes into if one is in Christ; it beggars description. The feeling that this brings into the soul — to be clean, no darkness at all, light as a feather — this lovely light...passing from the time dimension into eternity. It was a brief experience of what eternity will be like for those who are in Christ: joy unspeakable, a sense of being totally free from every bondage, for the first time to taste sheer, true happiness. It was very brief but amazing. I sensed the atmosphere of perfect peace and perfect happiness, almost exhilarating joy; but I did not see beings. There was a paean of worship which rose spontaneously from my spirit to Christ: pure adoration. I have no idea of why the experience was given. It just happened. Satan had often taunted about going into this paradise. It was as though God showed me the reality of it in this present existence. I suppose that is the quality of eternal life; the quality of it is pure. Eternal life is not just a matter of length of life.

40   *THE GLORY OF THE HEAVENLIES*

There was an outstanding occasion of an encounter with Christ when He completely cleansed me from sin and took me into eternity for a few moments. The Spirit said, 'I've to take you into the heavenlies, but you can't come with any spot or wrinkle. You must be utterly cleansed in the blood of Christ, or you will be totally wrecked in the heavenlies.' There swept through me in the briefest measurable space of time a sense of being totally clean. Like an eagle I was caught up on an uprising current of air, and there I met Christ — not as Son of Man, but as Son of God. I had been washed and had received eye salve and been enabled to see these things, and had been brought into a condition where I was not terrified. The natural human would be in a state of shock with close proximity to Christ unless He intervened and gave His covering.

The sudden revelation of His glory was given to my mother too just before her death, and all fear was taken. She became a spiritual being, and the greater attraction eclipsed the fear. In that minute, I believe, mother was born a spiritual creature.[1] She was afraid before because she was still earthly, born of the flesh. Now she wanted the spiritual.

Note

[1] Miss Taylor is here using the expression 'born a spiritual creature' in a special sense. She well knew and taught that at conversion a person was born again and in that sense became spiritual.

41 *THE HEAVENLIES AGAIN*

On the day of which I recently spoke (sec. 40), when I entered into the heavenlies, I felt I came as near as one may to looking on God. It was not a direct looking; it was a sensing of His presence, of an emanation of love. There was awe, a holy worshipping fear, and a knowledge of Christ at God's right hand. He had led me there and I was accepted in Him. Everything that had offended God had been taken away. I had sinned and known conviction before conversion. I too had seen the look that Peter saw. Through the years I never lost my love for Christ. Never was He downgraded in my consciousness.

But there came that one moment — a moment stolen out of time, which I will never forget. There was an awareness of the complete control God held over everything, which destroyed the apprehension of the unknown. One strong emanation from Christ was kindness, gentleness, a desire to love and be loved.

42 *SINGING OF ETERNITY*

I have heard the singing of eternity. Much that is on offer nowadays I feel is of Satan. There is no ragged, broken beat in eternal singing; the sound of its cadences is sweet and flowing. If you have caught it yourself you can transmit it. Music of the world is hideous by comparison.

Some wonder why in singing they don't get the spiritual output that others achieve. Singing is a spiritual thing, and mere mechanical correctness is no substitute for spirituality.

43 *HEAVEN WITH ITS MUSIC AND COLOUR*

Heaven is spiritual. It does not consist of definable objects. I am not impressed with some people's ideas about this. Heaven's objects don't come within the scope of natural thinking. It is the spiritual part of the person that can lay hold upon them, not the human part. It is the spacelessness and the timelessness that the human can't lay hold on. Spiritual people find themselves in their element. We have to be transformed before we can really appreciate this.

The atmosphere of music and colour is continuous. It is a feast for spiritual ears and eyes, as though someone had come up athirst from the desert and found themselves in a well-watered garden. The colour is pure, not the faded thing we have on earth, but vivid, alive, deep. In that sort of situation I began to see people in colour, for they are a part of that. The colours are wonderful, if you have a love of beauty, sight and sound. Nothing on earth gives any indication of the quality of the beauty, and yet it can come into the sound of singing here. I always waited for that tone in our own singing: the eternal beauty of sound. When it came I knew that the people were in touch with the eternal. It transcended the confines of time. Ugliness has a frightful effect on me, whether ugliness of temperament or form or feature; it is so foreign to the beauty of eternity. I believe that, in our passing over, God gives us eye salve to see these things; they are not seen by mortal vision. Christ is the personification, the acme, of beauty of sound and colour. Humans try to bring the eternal down to earth. God takes us upwards. He wants to lift us up to His eternity. We get there by being quiet and allowing His Spirit to purify our perception. You have got to be very still in your spirit to get the true reflection of things, undamaged by a ruffling of the water of mind or spirit.

To get into the eternal realm you have to be very deep in Christ — to the eclipsing of yourself, the thought life, everything.

44 *FURTHER REFLECTIONS ON COLOUR*

The colour comes from Christ Himself. Lights can be broken into colour as in a rainbow, or as the sun on dust creates colour. So Christ coming through the dust of humanity creates a colour of its own. It transforms the whole appearance of life. It is wonderful to see the basis of colour in its original depth, power and purity: it is not of earth.

It is 'personality', not an 'aura', in colour. Some people are transparent; that is when they are becoming really spiritual.

45 *SPIRITUAL LIGHT*

For about two weeks now G— has been bathed in the eternal light, clothed with light as man was in the beginning.

On one occasion in our Tuesday night prayer meeting, God's presence was almost tangible. I was speaking, and while speaking knew tremendous anointing. A great light came into the hall. Each one in the company became like a torch, lit from within, as though being prepared for the Rapture. A terrific change takes place. The natural is replaced by the spiritual as we enter true spiritual life, for those who are in Christ. There is a light that is power, and G— is the vehicle of transmission.[1]

There is a preparation for the greater glory of the latter day. I think it is imminent.

It is a lovely thing to see a person robed in light — the human part illuminated. You catch the faint outline of a spiritual being.

.   .   .   .   .

There came a moment before my grandmother died that her face was seen to be shining. There was no fear of passing over; being created a spiritual being she could hear the music and absorb it.[2]

.   .   .   .   .

[It may be relevant to add that Miss Taylor believed there was an angelic host on earth.]

Notes

[1] Miss Taylor went on to give me permission to communicate this.
[2] So clear was the shining that one of the family turned round, enquiring who had switched on a light!

46 *A TASTE OF HELL*

I saw hell at conversion and once or twice since. At conversion, while I was under dreadful, devastating conviction of sin and was crying out to God for help (it seemed a contradiction),[1] He took me to hell and showed me hell. And it was a complete separation from Himself. To know one is cut off forever from fellowship with Himself, from union with Himself, is hell.[2]

Another occasion was more like seeing than feeling. It was like a market square milling with people. There were little lanes going off from it and people coming in distraught, lost — they didn't know where to turn. They had no peace, no relief. Their faces were gaunt and haunted as they rushed from one point to another without direction, obviously in agony of mind and spirit. It put me in mind of a man trying to get into a house and not being able to find the door (as in the story of the men of Sodom, Gen 19:11). Oh, it was frightful — the hopelessness of it. It was so horrifying I told Mr Black at the time. The awful hopelessness.

Notes

[1] She was calling out to God, whose existence she had denied.
[2] On another occasion Miss Taylor described the experience of separation from God as being eternally cut off from a part of oneself — for one is not whole apart from Him.

47   PREPARING FOR THE HOMEGOING

In the past week I had a strong feeling that I was to go on. There was a strong desire to know Christ as He is, before meeting Him in eternity. I did not want anything of my own imagination; I wanted the real Christ. There came an overwhelming sense of His presence — the eternal Son of God. There was something new and different in this experience. It was not the result of my imagination working on something of my own. I was in a condition of abiding, neither trying anything nor asking any questions.

The child runs to the mother or father, whichever emanates love the more. With no question it runs to the parent and drinks in the quality of the parent's spirit: love, compassion, care, trustworthiness. It abides in the very nature of the parent, going past the form to the very essence of the parent's being.

48 *KNOWING WHAT GOD IS LIKE*

I have an increasing curiosity to know what God is like
as I am coming near to seeing Him face to face. We
would need to be changed from this body, wouldn't we,
to get a new sense of perception. When in the throes of
reaction to an antibiotic I went through something like
the process of dying.[1] It brought this sharply to mind.
(It was a very, very pleasant experience.) What form do
we actually meet? Christ said, 'He that hath seen me
hath seen the Father.' Did He mean the physical Jesus
or the spiritual Son of God? In my opinion it is God the
Son from eternity past. Anything physical is temporal.
We need to be changed to pass into the eternal. We
would be completely bewildered if we passed in as we
are.

Note

[1] Miss Taylor was allergic to penicillin. She is referring to an incident
that had happened about four nights previously.

49   HANDING DYING MOTHER OVER TO CHRIST

Tell H— that I think it could be for her to take her
mother out [in spirit] as I took Bertie and my mother
and handed them over to Christ.[1] There came a moment
when this actually happened. My part was finished.
H— should prepare herself and get so close to Christ
that this may happen. I particularly want her to know
this.

Note

[1] Bertie was a brother of Miss Taylor's. She basically meant that a person
could go out in spirit with another who was dying, to the point of
feeling a handing over of them to Christ in a very particular way.

50 COMMUNION OF SAINTS

I never lost touch with my mother's spirit.[1] The bond is much stronger than when she was alive. I am convinced that people gone on know what happens on earth, especially with those close to them. I never knew my father except as a small child, and so I didn't build a relationship with him as an adult spiritual being.

There is a thought transaction, not in words: a sense of the presence, but the presence is not there. There is no convergence on the natural world in a material form. I am quite sure there is no actual presence. They do not materialize.

On many occasions I have had a sense of my mother — I have been aware of her as a spiritual being.

Note

[1] I think Miss Taylor had real difficulty in communicating what she really felt about this subject. She found language limiting and wanted to avoid giving any wrong impression. She was totally opposed to seeking communication with the dead. She viewed spiritualism as a great evil. It is nevertheless true that she had clear consciousness of her mother as alive in another dimension. Scripture of course supports this view. The writer of the epistle to the Hebrews could say that 'we also are encompassed about with so great a cloud of witnesses' (Heb 12:1).

51 *THE VALLEY OF THE SHADOW*

Understand that this was an experience of the valley of the shadow and not of death itself. When I found myself really ill my first thoughts were to get you and J—, whose very presence is a ministering spirit — her presence brings a sense of healing to my spirit. Neither was available, and I felt cut off from normal means of succour. I felt desolate, actually. I need you as a leader for healing and endurance. I was feeling very low when the words of a psalm came: 'Yea, though I walk through the valley of the shadow of death...*thou* art with me.' There was an opening of heaven and a pouring out of the very presence of God. It was sufficient. The healing and quietness came into my spirit, and the sense of completion. There came with it a fresh emphasis on the words of Christ: 'I have prayed for you that your faith fail not.'

There has been an awful fear of failure at the end. Satan is working to undermine the very fundamentals of my faith in God and in the efficacy of the work of Calvary — making a dead set at that to destroy my confidence in His words that He will do what He said He would do, that there will be life, that death is the entrance to life for those who are in Christ. There came a complete peace on my spirit. It was triggered by the word *thou*: 'Thou art with me.' It was not just words, but factual experience. It was quite an experience: the realization that when human help was not available He was sufficient. This spilled over to the passing. I am not to be afraid, for He will be with me and Christ is praying that my faith will not fail. I think the closer you have lived systematically with God and the deeper and stronger your confidence in Him, the greater is the force with which Satan tries to match that. He tried to convince Christ that God had forsaken Him, just at the moment of His ultimate yielding to the unknown

(unknown to Jesus the man). Satan must have a fearful hatred of Christ: even at the last moment he wants to rob Him of the faith of His child. 'I will hide thee in the secret of my pavilion': K— was speaking of that this morning. That exactly fitted the situation on the night of the uproar (sec. 33).

I have an increasing realization of the words of Scripture, 'dwelling under the shadow of the Almighty' — living in God. When an emergency arises there is no emergency, but an abiding in Christ. The fact is we are living in God and we shall not be moved. It certainly means that secular life is brought under the domination of the Spirit of Christ.

Vision of a Work

52   *THE COMING OF VISION OF NEW WORK*

[Miss Taylor spoke of the beginning of the work which has developed into the Struthers movement. After describing events leading up to this, she continued as follows.]

In the house, sitting quietly, I sensed God's presence deepening. I listened to hear what the Holy Spirit had to say. The knowledge was given that God, the Trinity, had in mind to do something in particular. God was indeed to begin a work with a company of people who would propagate Pentecost. The Holy Spirit would be in His rightful place in the church: not 'it' but a Person honoured, listened to and obeyed. I thought this was marvellous — but He wanted me to be in charge of it. I felt I did not have the panache or the organizational ability.

'Lord, I couldn't do that. Could I have someone to be the public relations person?' I was wrong. God would have overruled my deficiencies. I asked if I could have someone, and He said, 'Yes.' I asked if it could be Mr Black, and this was granted. God said the new movement would be completely under His control: He would direct each step of the way. He would be in charge. Any change, He would make. There would be a standard for holiness, for purity of life, of word, of action. He would reveal the standard and we must not in any sense move from it or alter it. There was to be no lowering of the quality of life. Life would flow from the midst of ourselves; we would not become dependent on visiting speakers. The propagation of Pentecost was reiterated. The Holy Spirit was to have His proper place in the minds of the church of Christ on earth; the truth concerning Him was to be known. There was born in me a love for the Holy Spirit. Something happened: I seemed to meet Him and know Him.[1] There was a passionate love for Him but no diminution in my love for Christ.

I had lived a quiet backwater of a life. I foresaw the growth of a movement, and I was terrified. How would I meet strangers? I was so reserved that it was often an ordeal even to go shopping. Meeting people was not my forte. I realized that you [HB] would do this. I was trembling physically as I sat by the fireside. I contacted you.

You waited for a witness and said later, 'Yes, I feel there is a call.'[2]

Stage by stage, revelation came to me of what God wanted done.

Notes

[1] Compare Benny Hinn's attitude to the Holy Spirit as revealed in his *Good Morning, Holy Spirit* (Thomas Nelson, 1990; Word [U.K.], 1991).

[2] Miss Taylor's background was very different from mine, but in a strange way we had come to a similar position regarding the things of God. Through reading I knew of many of the principles of revival and really looked for a movement of the Wesleyan type combined with full Pentecost. I believed in the conviction and uncovering of sin, of deep repentance, sanctification and holiness and pentecostal power. I believed that a people could be moved to revival.

53 *THE CHARTER*

According to the charter given by God for the new work, there was to be holiness, Pentecost as in Acts, righteousness, truth, and a fearlessness of men. The Spirit said, 'There will be troubled waters, difficult times.' Though Satan would try to disrupt, we were not to be afraid. God was in charge; we were like the pieces on a chess board, and He would move the pieces. 'Ye shall be a sign spoken against.'[1] God's absolute purpose was and is and always shall be to give and teach others to give the Spirit His rightful place.

Note

[1] This was clearly predicted. Opposition and criticism would be fierce and very general.

54   *THE ORIGINAL VISION*

According to the revelation at the beginning, 'They are
mine. I will train them. I will feed them.' In the original
vision I saw a people separated unto Himself. We
would be a peculiar people unto God. He would guide,
direct and teach by His Spirit stage by stage, and no
stranger would teach His people. He would raise up
from the midst of the company those of His own
choice. There was to be a Holy Spirit people, a pentecostal people, brought into being for the propagation of
Pentecost. That was the purpose of the formation of the
church. This revelation came by knowledge, not in
visible form, in my own house.

55 *VISION OF THE FOUNTAIN*

There came a sense of being enclosed, shut in, the company assembled. Up from the centre of the hall, from a hole in the floor, a fountain sprang up very tall and spread very wide. It took in the whole company who were gathered. Revelation came: 'Even so will I make this church as a fountain taking in many people from many areas far beyond the centre.' There came a knowledge that the thing was already begun. It had started, and God was moving to perfect the revelation in fact.

[The fountain in this vision was very clearly identified with the mother church. The exact date of the vision is not recorded, but it was between 1962 and mid-1964. I noted that from that time almost everywhere I went (and I went to many places) was visited with blessing. Groups and churches formed and took root, e.g. Glasgow, Pudsey, Falkirk and Gorebridge. This vision too has been fulfilled, though it predated any sign of these things happening.]

56 *VISION OF CHILDREN'S WORK*

I saw a door where there is no door. The vision was on the platform wall of the church hall, towards the lane. I saw a doorway open. Christ was standing with His back against the lintel looking outwards. I saw Christ beckoning, although I shouldn't have been able to do so from that position.[1] I saw young people of all ages (starting with young adults), an innumerable host stretching as far as the eye could see — not a queue but a vast crowd. Christ was facing the lane, with His right hand towards the young people, beckoning them in. As they came He touched each one on the shoulder and guided them past Himself and into the hall, which was particularly bright and warm with a strong aroma of Christ, holiness, goodness and truth: that was the atmosphere He was bringing them into, out of the world.

At a later date (days or weeks later) came a revelation of knowledge that God would start with young adults, who at that time were a particular target of Satan. The youth of the world were being swept into an inferno by a fearfully powerful avalanche of sin. As with a forest fire one cuts a swathe to stop the inferno, so God wanted to do that, to be that ground of separation. He made a division in the horde going to hell, to stem the fierceness of onslaught and save some.

The first to be affected were the twenties' and older teens' group, up to the age of about thirty — then a Glasgow group started.

— I'll tell L — she is a brand plucked from the burning.

Yes, she is to stand in the gap, indeed (with her generation) to be the gap.

At a later date the same knowledge was given with regard to secondary school pupils and nearer the present time there came a tremendous surging, sweeping force of love of God for children before they should be contaminated. This in a sense was the most powerful of all: an intense, intense desire in the heart of God for young children before they were spoiled. He really opened the floodgates of His love to draw them, to attract them and give them a sense of security in Himself.[2]

Notes

[1] She had ability to see what natural vision would not have seen.

[2] I was in the hall when this vision came to Miss Taylor. Having felt withdrawn from the company during a time of prayer I sat alone with my back to the wall on the south side. I felt revelation pouring over me about ways and means of getting children of primary school age into church. In speaking to Miss Taylor later I realized that this had been happening to me while she had seen her vision. Until that point I had not been particularly interested in directing effort towards the age group indicated.

57 *VISION OF THE CHURCHES*

[The vision of the churches was received at the end of the last morning service at a Wiston camp. Miss Taylor described the vision in detail then. I was standing beside her at the top of the hall facing north. The anointing was tremendous, and Miss Taylor went prostrate before God. She saw almost a repeat of the vision of young people given earlier in the Greenock church, but now it was a vision of churches: churches of various descriptions stretching in all directions as far as eye could see. Some were complete buildings, some in process of being built. It was actually true at that time — not only brick and mortar but living stones. There was a connection between the central church and each branch. As the pipes fed from the olive tree into lamps (Zech 4:2–3), life was coursing into the branch churches, the same life. There was no difference between central and branches in quality of life. The standard was the same. The churches were of different sizes and shapes, situated in all directions, north, south, east and west. They would last until Christ returns. Through the years we have seen progressive stages in the literal fulfilment of this vision.]

While speaking once in Greenock I was so conscious of Christ standing behind me that I half turned to my left. He was standing in the pulpit leaning over toward the congregation. He held out His right hand in blessing and claimed the company for Himself. The back windows of the church became illumined with tremendous brightness and colour. There is an immense amount of colour in spiritual things. This was a beautiful revelation, which I often relived as I sat in the church. There again, as with the vision of young children coming in, there was a tremendous outflow of the love of God.

II

A TESTIMONY TO COMMITMENT

A TESTIMONY TO COMMITMENT

[This is the testimony of a lady whom we shall call X —, who at the age of twenty came into a place of deep and lasting commitment to Christ. It is followed by very significant remarks from Miss Taylor.]

X — 's Testimony

For the past few weeks, I had been feeling a very deep hunger and thirst for God — a hunger and thirst that I had never known in my Christian life before. I found that no matter how much God blessed me in each meeting, no matter how near He came, and how much Christ was revealed to me, it didn't satisfy me; it just wasn't enough. A few nights ago during our Saturday night meeting I felt that God was showing me a new depth, a new realm, that He would take me into. That night there were quite a few people seeing Miss Taylor, and so I decided I would see her on the following Monday night. But it was nearly the early hours of Tuesday morning by the time everybody else had been interviewed, and I wasn't quite sure what exactly I was going to say to Miss Taylor. I decided to go in anyway, and we spoke very briefly; I told her that I just wasn't satisfied. The revelation I was getting of Christ was glorious, but it wasn't enough. There was something more that I needed. So she nodded and said, 'Well, we'll pray.'

We turned to prayer, and Miss Taylor laid hands on me and ministered to me. She was speaking words from God, but I sensed that there was an area that she was speaking about which I couldn't grasp; I just couldn't understand it. It was as though she could see what God wanted to do in me and what He was doing; I sensed it was glorious, and I was praising Him for it. But I couldn't really grasp it; I couldn't fully understand it. While I was praising God, in my heart I was saying, 'But there's something else there. There's something that I just can't understand.'

And then all of a sudden something wonderful happened. The only way I can describe it is to say it was as though a whole building came down on top of me. In a split second the realization came of the truth and reality of the words which Miss Taylor was speaking, the words from God, and what Christ was doing within me at that moment. It was glorious. I suppose I always thought that He could, and would, do that in other people, but I never thought about it for me. I never thought that He could come in in such depth. I remember at first I was dumb — for a couple of seconds I literally couldn't say a word. I wanted to praise God, but couldn't say a single thing. I was attempting to speak and just nothing came out! And then after a few seconds it did come out, and I was praising God. The knowledge of what He was doing, and the full force of the realization of the words that Miss Taylor was speaking, were wonderful. She had understood beforehand what God was doing in me, but I just couldn't grasp it. It really did take a work of God to open up my mind and spirit to see what He had done. I felt tremendous, and ever since then it has been glorious. The best thing of all has been the revelation of Christ Himself. I just can't put into words what an outstanding experience it was at the time, and it didn't stop on Monday night; it has been ongoing. I have felt a new power and strength within me, and a deeper desire for God. I'm still not satisfied! I want more! But it's a healthy sort of hunger that I've got, and I praise God for it. As I have said, I knew God did work that way in other people, but I never thought of it happening in me. I knew He could do it, but I didn't know if He would. But He did it, and I do praise and thank Him for it; it was incredible.

Dialogue

HB: Wait a minute, X — . There are one or two points that I haven't got quite clear. Was there not a stage where you were prepared to commit your life to God absolutely and totally?

X — : Oh, yes.

HB: Don't you think that might be an important factor? In other words, I think many people suppose that they can come and get the riches of God without deep commitment. They think something just happens. I don't think they all realize the connection between total commitment and wonderful blessing. What about that side of it?

X — : You mean, when did I make my commitment?

HB: Yes.

X — : Two years ago, I remember God showing me a level of commitment where everything that I was at that time and ever would be should be given to Him. But then I saw a level within me at New Year time which I hadn't committed to God. I had thought I had, but this was a very fundamental part of me, and it was very, very hard. God has been, as it were, sort of chipping away at that block ever since then. It has been very difficult at times, but it has been glorious. It has been worth every minute of it.

HB: So by the time you had this experience with Miss Taylor there was nothing at all in life you were holding back?

X — : No, nothing. There is nothing that was worth holding back.

Miss Taylor Comments

I don't think X— has given a proper telling of what happened before the night of the breakthrough. When she came into the room, the first words she said were: 'I'm giving literally everything to God. I'm holding nothing to myself.' Now lots of people say that. But when she said it, there came an atmosphere, a presence, into the room. It was registered in heaven. She meant it. It wasn't something she was saying on the spur of the moment; it wasn't an emotional outburst. It was a considered statement. And as Mr Black says, there are so many people who think that they can come to God and ask for an experience and perforce they shall have it. But as I remarked earlier to Mr Black when we had been speaking about these things, 'It's like reading the story of revival. You get the end of it; you get what comes out of it. But on very, very few occasions do you get the homework, do you get what is behind revival in private lives.' And it was very important what X— had done in her homework before she came on that Monday. There is something essentially ours to do. I don't know how I can stress this sufficiently. There is an uttermost commitment to God. We either give that or we don't. We can have a pretence. But God knows when it is uttermost.

What happened at that stage on Monday night reminded me very, very much of my own moment of commitment. It was very like it. There was a looking into future life. I was quite a young woman at the time. I looked into the future and I said, 'Lord, the future is yours absolutely, unconditionally. Do with me what you will.' And I meant it. There was not one shred of reservation in any aspect of life, not a shred of reservation. The same thing happened on Monday night. There came a moment when X— committed herself irrevocably to God. God knows when that happens. He listens to our verbal commitment. It may be genuine at a level. But there comes a moment when it is absolute, *and we mean it.* And something happens. Only in that moment can it happen. We speak so much about commitment: 'I've committed my life to God' — and often even I know the person has not committed his or her life to God, in many cases. There are comparatively few in this hall tonight who have done that: comparatively few. But in the moment that that happens, there is a registering of it in heavenly places, and it is irrevocable, it is glorious. A load lifts off, doesn't it? A load of responsibility lifts off the spirit.

While the commitment is spiritual, it is nevertheless made in the cold-blood, unemotional action of our will. You see, when that happens, every detail of life is left in God's hands. I mean literally every detail of life. In whose hands could it be in better charge? Who can more wisely and with more love work out our life in time and in eternity? Our thinking, our speaking, our action, our ambition — they go. The mind of Christ comes in. And there is a transformation under this operation of the mind of Christ. That point was vital before the other could happen. We may deceive ourselves, but we cannot deceive God.

As the time went on, as God spoke, there came the knowledge that there was a scripture which He meant to fulfil. 'It pleased God the Father to reveal Christ in me.' These are the words of Paul. Now Paul wasn't beginning his Christian walk. He had served God, had served Christ, for a long time. Christ had been revealed to him. But there came this moment when he realized it had pleased God the Father to reveal Christ *in* him. And that is what happened on Monday night. On one occasion Christ said, 'The words which I speak unto you are spirit'. And in the transaction which happened in that room on that night, Christ was revealed in the centre core of that life. It was like a sunburst. I know the moment it happened — and as I have often said, I don't know whether the recipient or the one through whom the power is passing gets the greater blessing.

Christ, the literal Son of God, was revealed in a human life. *In*, not *to*. She's not looking *at* Christ. He is revealed *in* her. Now you can't understand that properly until it happens. It transforms life, spiritual and natural. It is an act of God. I do praise God for those in whom it has happened. But by comparison with the number of people *to* whom Christ is revealed, they are a very small number. Why? Because so many will not come into the place where it can happen. We skim along so happily. God is blessing, we have a tremendous sense of His presence, and life is good, it is sweet. And we fail to realize that there is a far, far greater glory to be revealed. We may go from strength to strength, from glory to glory — not our glory, not our being glorious more and more and more, but the revelation of the glory of God to increasing revelation of that glory. It is for every one who is born again: *for every one*. This is what God holds out to each of us, if we give Him our life by an act of the will, literally, actually, in cold blood. We have no more fancies then about what is happening to us, and what is not happening, what should happen, and what hasn't happened that ought to have happened. This goes completely, and there is a straight line through into the place which God has prepared for those who love Him. And it's not away up like the proverbial pie in the sky. The things which God has prepared for those who love Him are revealed unto us by the Holy Spirit: for those who love Him, to the exclusion of themselves. You should try it; it is wonderful. Thank you.

Mr Black Comments

Could I add to that same subject perhaps one word of warning. Spiritual experiences are remarkably different, and sometimes when you hear a testimony you think, 'Ah, it didn't happen to me that way.' Well, just remember, when you hear a testimony to salvation, have you ever heard two that were identical? Their differences don't make them any the less real. And you will find that people come into the deeps of which Miss Taylor has been speaking, in different ways. I mean by that, the actual detail of the spiritual experience varies from person to person. You may say, 'It didn't happen to me exactly the way it seems to have happened to X —,' but that doesn't mean that it hasn't happened to a limited number of you. Now don't go trying to copy the details of somebody else's spiritual experience. That way lies real difficulty. God has a pathway that is perfect for you. He has a road for you that is different from everyone else's. It is not so much how you come; it is the Person to whom you come, and the depth at which you come. Come to that full and absolute commitment of which Miss Taylor has been speaking, and leave the next step in His hand, the outworking of the detail. Your experience will be peculiarly your own, with features that are yours and nobody else's. In Miss Taylor's own case, on that street she made that commitment, and she did not immediately go into the ecstasy which X — knew in a very few moments. These things do not always work exactly the same way.

III

THE LOST HORIZON

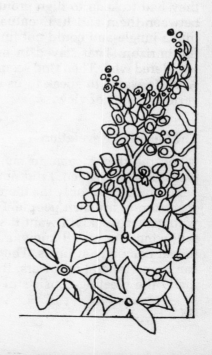

THE LOST HORIZON

A sermon preached on 14 March 1982

Recently there came back to my mind the title of a book which I came across very many years ago. I don't remember the story accurately, but the title included the words *Lost Horizon*, and, as far as I can recall, the story was of a group of men who went exploring to find what was beyond the horizon at the edge of the world.

The definition of *horizon* is 'the circle bounding the view where earth and heaven appear to meet'. Now this is an absolutely secular definition — but is it? *Where earth and heaven appear to meet...*

They set out to find the horizon, and to arrive there they had to keep to high ground where nothing came between them and it. Eventually they got themselves into a jungle and could not find the way out: they lost the horizon. That stayed in my consciousness, and I wondered why. Then God seemed to touch the thought. And He wants to speak to us about the horizon, from various points of view.

The Opening Revelation

When the theme came to me, I wondered when God wanted it to be given. I did not know what the sermon would be; I knew only the theme. Then He said, 'I want it spoken to my own people. I want it spoken to those who gather weekly; I want it spoken to those who are following.' As we all know, a Saturday night can be a mixed company at times. There can be unsaved, there can be peripheral followers. But on Sunday night normally the meeting consists of those who have started on the journey at least. God is coming very close to us as a church, as a part of the body of Christ — for me, at times, 'frighteningly' close (for want of a better word). Now by that I don't mean a terror filling my soul, but 'frightening' in the sense of the awesomeness of God drawing so close, drawing so near. There comes an awe, a fear of the lesser for the greater. There comes with this awareness of His drawing near an increasing consciousness of who He is. He is God, He is the Lord God of Hosts, He is the Creator of all that is. He is holding the world at this moment in space. He is keeping us alive in this present time. He is causing our lungs and hearts to function; He is feeding and clothing us. 'Oh,' we may say, 'I work and earn wages and buy my own food and clothes.' Originally it comes by the permissive will and the providence of God. We are utterly dependent on God for everything — literally everything. Dependent on Him who can supply and who can withold, who can create and who can destroy: God. He is drawing very, very close to the church of Christ at this time, and, thanks be to God, to this part of the church of Christ. Or *is* it 'Thanks be to God' in your heart?

A Lost Horizon

When God created the human race, he put Adam in a situation where he had a clear view of a specific horizon. Adam was created innocent, and God's purpose was that by a progression of choices he would become holy. In that moment he would be joined with God in the holiness of the Trinity: man would be brought into that relationship. Holiness is God, is the nature of God, is that which emanates from God alone. And God had set a horizon for Adam, that he should aim towards that place where earth and heaven met, in the true sense. But we know what happened. Adam went into a forest; Adam went into a jungle of sin. It's so easy to go into the jungle or the forest. It is much easier than keeping that straight road with a clear view through to the horizon that God set before man, where earth and heaven merge.

Mankind lost the horizon. We read in Isaiah:

> Behold, their valiant ones cry without: the ambassadors of peace weep bitterly. The high ways lie waste, the wayfaring man ceaseth: he hath broken the covenant, he hath despised the cities, he regardeth not man. The land mourneth and languisheth: Lebanon is ashamed and withereth away: Sharon is like a desert; and Bashan and Carmel shake off their leaves (Is 33:7–9).

And we come to this condition into which the human race descended. The sights, the sounds seem initially to be very attractive. Adam didn't mean to strip the tree and eat all the fruit. He just intended to taste it: he had never tasted it before. It was new. He didn't know what it would be like. 'I'll just have a bite.' That was all.

Now man doesn't go into sin headlong, intending to become filthy, corrupt. Man just thinks, 'I'll take a little taste. It couldn't possibly do me any harm. I've no intention of going deeply into sin. But it's new, it's different; I haven't tasted it before in this particular form.'

'The high ways lie waste.' That bite, that fruit, that deviation brought the human race into the place of a jungle. There was poison in that bite. And the mind of man was poisoned. The horizon disappeared. He lost sight of where God had planned his journey to end.

A New Horizon

We start off at Calvary, and God shows us that horizon, where the earthly meets and merges into the heavenly: a new life, a new direction, a clear way, a new focal point. We see right through in Christ. Where are you, where am I, now? Where are those of us who did come to Christ, those of us to whom God showed that original horizon as he showed it to Adam, that horizon, that circle? You see, many people who take a little journey, a few steps, in a devious way into a side pathway, think, 'Well, the horizon's a circle. It doesn't matter which direction I take; I'm bound to come out to it somewhere.'

New Distractions

How sinful is sin! How deceitful is sin! In the story the people went round and round and round in the jungle. The compass wasn't working properly. The compass was broken. And those of us who came to Christ, those of us to whom He gave a direction, had our compass set on a straight path to that horizon. In reaching that point there would be a merging into what lay beyond. Have we broken our compass? Do we find it as delightful, do we find it as precious, this journeying straight toward that point that was indicated at the cross? A new life, a clean life, a different life? Methinks there are many of us who have taken little forays into the jungle. Such are present in every company; perhaps every one of us at some time has strayed in this way. 'Oh, we're not going too far. But it's lovely to see the sun shining through the trees. It looks beautiful in there. There's a lovely scent. Let's just find out what it is.'

They are very attractive: the things of the world, the pleasures of the flesh, of the natural being. Now I don't say that the world is a horrible place and that there is no pleasure in it. To the carnal being there are pleasures in sin, there are delights in sin, there are attractions in sin — strong attractions, very nice to look at, touch, taste — whatever form they might take. The delights of the carnal world can be considerable. There is no point in saying to people, 'Come out of the world; it's a horrible place, and you'll never have pleasure or happiness there.' That is not true, and has to be qualified. To the carnal mind (albeit claiming salvation), there are pleasures in sin, in this world. 'Just a little taste, just a little while, an hour or two, shouldn't really make any difference. I don't mean to spend the rest of my life in a social round; I don't mean to spend the rest of my life in following out this pastime. Just an hour or two, a day or two.' But the poison comes in, as the poison came into Adam. And we are blinded; we can't read the compass; we are lost. That first step, seemingly so innocuous, was the first step towards losing the horizon. The tragedy of the Christian who has lost the horizon that God set before His born-again people! They now can have pleasure. They have forgotten all about the horizon. The carnal has taken over where the spiritual should have reigned. The natural mind has largely taken over the aims, purposes and pleasures of the being.

> Behold, their valiant ones cry without: the ambassadors of peace weep bitterly. The high ways lie waste, the wayfaring man ceaseth: he hath broken the covenant...

'He hath broken the covenant.' What did we say when we came to Christ, to God through Christ at Calvary, in that moment when in the popular phrase we 'accepted Christ into our heart'? What did we say? 'Lord, I give You my life. If You will forgive me my sin I will be Yours for ever.' We made a covenant with God, and it was sealed with the blood of Christ. Are we keeping the covenant? Have we kept the covenant? Man breaks the covenant, not God. God is speaking to us every one without exception. What are we doing with the covenant we made with God in Christ? — 'Give me salvation, cleanse me from my sin, and I promise to be faithful to You. I give my life to You.'

> The land mourneth and languisheth: Lebanon is ashamed and withereth...

Divine Reaction

And what is God thinking about this? This church that has lost the horizon? These members of the church who have lost the horizon, perhaps I should say more correctly? What is God purposing to do — what has he done in time past? What will He do in time present and time future? To continue in that same chapter:

> Now will I arise, saith the LORD; now will I lift up myself; now will I be exalted. Ye shall conceive chaff, ye shall bring forth stubble: your breath is a fire that shall devour you. And the peoples shall be as the burning of lime: as thorns cut down, that are burned in the fire (vv. 10–12).

It seems a fearful destruction; it seems as though it is a vengeance that God is pouring out upon those who have broken His covenant. It can be so. But there is another sense in which God is speaking in the present time in this context. What will He do? He will pour out the fire of His Holy Spirit. Oh, blessed be His name! He will purge with fire; He will purify the life that comes again to Him, that returns to Him, the life that realizes it is lost in a jungle of sin, that it has broken the covenant it made with God at Calvary. We are having opportunity to turn about and to be restored. We are being given opportunity to rediscover the horizon. Can you understand, child of God? You who are living a semi-spiritual — a carnal spiritual life? A carnal spiritual life? I am not blind, I am not stupid, I am not starry-eyed about the congregations of this present day, either in our own movement or out of it. He will send His fire.

...now will I lift up myself; now will I be exalted.

God is offering another opportunity to find the horizon. Do you want to find the original horizon? Or have you broken the compass and thrown it away? 'I don't want to know what's beyond the horizon.' Is that what you're saying? 'I'm not interested.' Then God help us, any who are in that condition. When the outpouring of the Holy Spirit comes upon the church of Christ, as it is coming, we shall know the purging, purifying fire of God. As brimstone it shall fall upon the church of Christ. He shall burn up the dross, because He shall present to the Father a church without blemish, without spot, without wrinkle or any such thing. If you love your blemish, if you love your spot, your wrinkle, God help you in that day — for you will have taken yourself out from underneath the covering of His love. He has spoken and is speaking to us: 'Repent, come to Me. Turn ye again unto Me, and I will receive you.' He has been saying it for many days. 'Come out from among them and be ye separate, saith the Lord God of Hosts.' Come out from among them and be ye separate. 'Touch not the unclean thing.'

Sinners in Zion

God is speaking to us. The church of Christ is holy, is sacred, is the body of Christ. Do you realize what you have done in taking to yourself the name of the Lord Jesus Christ? Do you realize what you have done in making a covenant with God? You became part of the body of Christ, born of God. And God says that in that day the church of Christ, the bride of Christ, shall be without blemish, without spot, wrinkle or any such thing. It won't be left to you, to me, to decide whether we'll hold on to this little peccadillo, this hour of pleasure, this way of self-pleasing. It won't be left to you, or to me. God will purge, and it will be painful. It will be searing. God is speaking to the church of Christ; God is speaking to the people who are claiming to be part of the body, the bride of Christ. You cannot, by any stretch of the imagination, deceive God.

> Hear, ye that are far off, what I have done; and, ye that are
> near, acknowledge my might. The sinners in Zion are
> afraid (vv. 13–14).

Oh, yes, the sinners in Zion! The members of the body
of Christ shall fear with an horrible fearing when the
outpouring of the Holy Spirit is upon the church as
God shall pour it in the last days, in the day of utter
cleansing, of utter purification.

> ...trembling hath surprised the godless ones. Who among
> us shall dwell with the devouring fire? Who among us
> shall dwell with everlasting burnings? (v. 14)

Who of us? Let me say it again. Make sure you are born
again. You who delight in sin, you who walk far off
from God, you who at this moment are defying God: it
shall not always be that way. The burnings of God shall
come upon the church which is His bride. He will not
suffer pollution to be in her. She cannot appear before
Him with a spot. Are you born again? I ask you. Oh, you
have gone through a form of 'Yes, I believe.' You have
gone through a form of Christianity. It's wearing thin,
very thin. What is showing through? A carnal life is
showing through, which is anathema to God. Sin in the
church of Christ is anathema to God. And it will not be
lightly forgiven. It is trampling again underfoot the
blood of Christ. Oh, that the church of Christ would
have one moment's realization of the value of the blood
of Christ to God. You would know then whether you
are free to do as you please. A pseudo-spirituality, a
pseudo-Christianity, the name of Christ and 'I do what I
like. I don't see any harm in doing this, I don't see any
harm in doing that; I don't see why *my* life should be
ordered by the church.' In other words, you won't face
up to it that it is God that is ordering the course of life,
and you say, 'I don't have to do what she says, I don't
have to do what he says. I will do what I think.' Oh, so

clear and safe, so safe! I say no, God says no, it's not safe. God has spoken.

Every one of us who has taken upon us the name of the Lord Jesus Christ, every one of us who has made a covenant of rebirth with God through Christ, shall answer before God in time and in eternity. Don't think that you will make your own way. The man who went into the wedding with his own garment, which he thought was better than the one that the host had provided, didn't make much of it, did he? He was turned out! He had been invited to the wedding. Will it be that some of us in that day shall hear the words, 'Depart from Me; I never knew you.' 'Oh, but we did this in Your name, and we did that in Your name.' 'Depart...I never knew you.' Don't live in a fool's paradise — don't. Salvation is holy, salvation is sacred, salvation is the life of Christ, the gift of God. What does it mean to each of us that we have received that priceless gift from God? What does it mean?

The Choice

A life that is lived in the joy of His presence, or a life that is lived to please myself: 'Well, Lord, I came to You through Christ, so it's all right. You can't put me in hell.' Can't He? 'No man shall pluck them out of my hand' — yes, but I can take myself out of the hand of God. I can take myself out of the security of salvation. I can sin away my day of grace. Too late, too late, shall be the cry. 'I mean to make things all right before I die...*but I'm dead — I'm over the line!*' Shall it be?

Were you thinking, 'I'm not going to change. I like my life; I'm having it my way'? — like that song that you hear so often (it drives me almost crazy): 'I did it my way.' All right: let's do it our way. And we'll be like the man who went into the wedding feast his way. We'll find we are turned out. There is only one way: God's way. Only one way. Oh, this soft peddling of sin! For centuries, generations and generations, this teaching in the church of Christ, this easy, soft option: 'Enjoy yourself, there's nothing wrong; man was meant to enjoy himself.' Yes, man was — in God, not in carnality, not in sin. 'Touch not the unclean thing.' *Touch* not: not a touch! Come out, be separate, touch not. It doesn't say, 'Revel not'; it doesn't say, 'Indulge not.' It says, 'Touch not' — not even a touch.

Oh, if one could realize how sacred is the body of Christ, the church of Christ, the born-again church of Christ, how precious it is to God, how jealous He is for the purity of the bride of Christ! Oh, that we had more apostolic teaching and preaching! That those who would preach the truth would call sin sin, would tell people just where we are! The majority of Christians have lost the way. We don't know where we are going. Sometime we're going somewhere and it will be happy and it will be lovely — but — 'I'm going my own way.' We may not find our way out of the jungle: we may never again see the horizon. But God is giving opportunity. God is speaking in this day, in this hour, this time. God is warning. And in this place, in these days, in this hour, there are those who are doing exactly what the people did who lived in the time of Noah.

They said,

'You've been telling us this for a long while. It hasn't happened...

'It's a longer time now since you started talking; it still hasn't happened. It won't happen in my time.'

It won't happen in our time? It will happen, nevertheless, and we shall all be in eternity, where the consequence of our earth life will be revealed.

The horizon is still there. That place where earth and heaven meet and merge is still there. But we have got to walk where we can see, where there is nothing blocking the view. We have got to walk where there is a wide vista of seeing. The clear through-way — not towers and scented bowers of our own pleasure, but a vast, open space, a life that is cleared of the hindering things, the unclean things, the sights, the sounds, the attractions of sin. Walking in the high places:

> Lord, lift me up, and let me stand,
> By faith, on heaven's tableland

— high above. Are you walking the highway? 'A highway shall be there, and a way.' It's still there. It's a highway: it's above sin. 'The wayfaring man, yea, though a fool, will not err therein.' Are you grovelling in the lowlands? Are you grovelling among the trees, the bushes, the darkness? 'Oh, there's sun over here,' and we rush over. 'It will be better here — oh, no, it's better over there — we'll go over there. Let's try this, let's try that, let's try the next thing.'

Are you walking above the forest, your eyes focused on that circle, God's promise? What lies *beyond* the horizon? beyond a regained, a rediscovered horizon? Now don't let's get tied up with words. I can say that never, never did I speak, never was I used of God, with such deep conviction of the knowledge that God is speaking to some in particular, as I am now. To those who are living a carnal spiritual life, or should I say a carnal Christian life, God is offering to adjust the compass, to bring out of the forest of sin, that again you may stand in that place of clear vision, of far seeing. God is here. God is speaking.

Beyond the horizon

That which lies beyond the horizon has no attraction for the carnal Christian: none at all. Let me repeat: I am not blind, I am not stupid. I am extremely perceptive. And I know that in a company such as this to which I now preach there are those to whom beyond the horizon has no interest. What lies beyond is not even thought about. It is of so little consequence that it has no place in the plan of their life, the life that they are living their way. They don't want to hear that which is beyond the veil. They don't want to hear about that which is beyond the temporal world. They don't want to hear about that which goes alongside the temporal world, where the temporal world is blotted out because the spiritual has superseded it. 'I don't want it.' I know you don't want it. I am not hoodwinked; neither is God. You give lip service, and your heart is far away. It's written in your eyes, it's written in your faces; you are read like a book. There is no covering. All things are known, are revealed, to God, and to those to whom He reveals them.

It is not a word of condemnation unto death — praise His name. It is a word of condemnation unto life — that that which is under condemnation shall be put away, and that life, eternal life, the life of Christ, shall enter into the place you promised to give when you took His salvation. You made an exchange — or you pretended to. You pretended to, or did you?

The Voyage of the Dawn Treader

I want to read a few excerpts from *The Voyage of the Dawn Treader*, one of C. S. Lewis' Narnia books.[1] These books are a species of fact clothed in fiction. They bring us very near to truth in a very lovely way — this one in particular. Very recently it suddenly came into my mind. In the story the young people aboard the ship called the *Dawn Treader* were looking and aiming for the horizon. But there was one on that ship who wasn't aiming merely to arrive at the horizon; he was aiming to go over, to cross. (They are really wonderful books in the way that they bring out deep spiritual truths.) At this stage they are travelling towards the very end, or physical limit, of the world. They are seeking to find what is 'over the edge'. But little Reepicheep is quite confident of what is beyond the horizon. They are aiming for where we may aim: to find what is beyond the horizon. As I say, Reepicheep knew: deep in his being he knew. He'd caught a glimpse.

> ...by this time the *Dawn Treader* was gliding over a part of the sea which seemed to be uninhabited.

When we start out in reality to find 'beyond the horizon', we are not going through crowds. We are not trying to find a place amongst the multitude. I don't think we would find much difficulty, those of us who are wanting to find 'beyond the horizon'; I don't think we'd find it very difficult to make our way in view of the small number of us who are going. You see, I'm not speaking poetic nonsense, sentimental slush. God has indicated that beyond that horizon, which is as far as we can see, there is that which we cannot see. How many of us are journeying straight for the horizon that we might cross it — in reality, now? How many of us are voyaging on the *Dawn Treader*? Which is more real to you? That which is to be discovered beyond the horizon, or what will happen tomorrow when we go to work or school or wherever we are going? Which is more real? I wonder how many of us have this one objective: to cross the horizon where earth and heaven meet? To cross it is to go into heaven. 'Oh, we're all going there.' Oh, no, we're not.

> ...for many days...the *Dawn Treader* glided smoothly east. Every day and every hour the light became more brilliant and still they could bear it. No one ate or slept and no one wanted to, but they drew buckets of dazzling water from the sea, stronger than wine and somehow wetter, more liquid, than ordinary water, and pledged one another silently in deep draughts of it. [Some of those who had been older] grew younger every day. Everyone on board was filled with joy and excitement, but not an excitement that made one talk. The further they sailed the less they spoke, and then almost in a whisper. The stillness of that last sea laid hold on them.

Child of God, are you there? Have you stopped talking? Talking about, talking to, talking with — talk, talk, talk. We stop dead. And as you draw nearer, in that last sea, when you draw near, you stop talking. It is too deep for sound.

A Sea of Whiteness

'My Lord,' said Caspian to Drinian one day, 'what do you see ahead?'

'Sire,' said Drinian, 'I see whiteness. All along the horizon from north to south, as far as my eyes can reach.'

'That is what I see too,' said Caspian, 'and I cannot imagine what it is.'

Whiteness. That horizon that God has set before us is white — is pure.

'If we were in higher latitudes, your Majesty,' said Drinian, 'I would say it was ice. But it can't be that; not here...'

...The whiteness did not get any less mysterious as they approached it. If it was land it must be a very strange land, for it seemed just as smooth as the water and on the same level with it. When they got very close to it Drinian put the helm hard over and turned the *Dawn Treader* south so that she was broadside on to the current and rowed a little way southward along the edge of the whiteness...

And still no one could make out what the white stuff was. Then the boat was lowered and it put off to investigate. Those who remained on the *Dawn Treader* could see that the boat pushed right in amidst the whiteness. Then they could hear the voices of the party in the boat (clear across the still water) talking in a shrill and surprised way.

Then the boat came back full

of the white stuff inside her. Everyone crowded to the side to hear the news.

'Lilies, your Majesty!'

Whiteness, purity, the horizon. It is not just a story. That horizon that God set before us, that is still before us if we want it, is white, is pure.

> And when, after some consultation, the *Dawn Treader* turned into the current and began to glide eastward through the Lily Lake or Silver Sea (they tried both these names, but it was the Silver Sea that stuck and is now on Caspian's map) the strangest part of their travels began.

Now grasp it: this is you, this is me, approaching that horizon that God has set, that white, that pure horizon where earth and heaven meet.

> Very soon the open sea which they were leaving was only a thin rim of blue on the western horizon. Whiteness, shot with faintest colour of gold, spread round them on every side, except just astern where their passage had thrust the lilies apart and left an open lane of water that shone like dark green glass. To look at, this last sea was very like the Arctic; and if their eyes had not by now grown as strong as eagles' the sun on all this whiteness — especially at early morning when the sun was hugest — would have been unbearable.

The increasing light. As we approach God's horizon, the purity, the fragrance, light — light unapproachable. That's where we're going: that's the horizon to which God is drawing us! Have you seen it? Do you see it? Is it calling? Are your eyes still holden? So strong that had our eyes not been made strong as eagles' we could not bear it: blinded by the brilliance of the light of His glory.

> And every evening the same whiteness made the daylight last longer. There seemed no end to the lilies. Day after day from all those miles and leagues of flowers there rose a smell which Lucy found it very hard to describe; sweet — yes, but not at all sleepy or overpowering, a fresh, wild, lonely smell that seemed to get into your brain and make

you feel that you could go up mountains at a run or wrestle with an elephant. She and Caspian said to one another, 'I feel that I can't stand much more of this, yet I don't want it to stop.'

Are you there, child of God? Is that your experience at this moment? Is this where you are living? Is this what is filling your vision, your seeing? Are your eyes filled with this (so inadequate) description of God's horizon? As we approach the glory of the dwelling place of God, as we draw nearer and nearer, the whiteness, the purity, the fragrance, the light, is dazzling. Except we had been strengthened, we could not bear it. But we don't want it to stop. Do you know what I am talking about? Or might it just as well be Greek? This is what God has provided. This is the place to which we are journeying — or are we? 'I don't want it. I'd rather have the smelly, earthy life that I've chosen.' Or rather, 'O God, take this smelly earthiness from me. Take this from my eyes. Set my compass again, O God, that my journeying be toward the light, that my *Dawn Treader*, the ship on which I am, may be heading not just for, but straight into, the light beyond the horizon.'

There came a day when they had to row out of the current and feel their way forward at a snail's pace, rowing. And soon it was clear that the *Dawn Treader* could sail no further east...

'Friends,' said Caspian, 'we have now fulfilled the quest on which you embarked.'

We have found the horizon!

'The quest is ended. We all return. Get the boat up again.'

Crossing the Horizon

Have you, perchance, reached the horizon — and turned back? The crew and passengers on board this ship reached the horizon and said, 'Our quest is ended: we have found the horizon. We will go back.' Have you seen the glory of God? Have you had a flash of revelation — and said, 'That'll do. I'll go back now. Back to the life I have lived, back to the place I was, back to my carnal Christianity which is under the condemnation of God'? You are not ignorant any longer. God has spoken. God has told you what He has prepared for you. You cannot say, 'Well, if I had known it would be so wonderful I wouldn't have turned back.' You know (or may know, if you will know) what God is drawing the church into. And you are choosing now what you are doing about His offer. You are choosing at this moment carnality or purity. You are choosing whether to turn your boat and go back, if you have even started a little way on that journey, or to go on. It attracts or it does not attract. Oh, child of God, how wonderful to be in Christ Jesus, travelling towards that horizon. Near enough now to see the whiteness, near enough to smell the fragrance. Whiteness of Christ, fragrance of Christ, glory of God, nearer and nearer and nearer. Where are you?

'Sire,' said Reepicheep, 'we do not *all* return.'

He had no intention of returning: he was going through. He was crossing, crossing the horizon. He wanted to be beyond it, once and for ever, beyond — out from this life of sin, this life of carnality, into the glory of the presence of God.

Then up came the sun, and at its first rising they saw it through the wall and it turned into wonderful rainbow colours. Then they knew that the wall was really a long, tall wave — a wave endlessly fixed in one place as you may often see at the edge of a waterfall... You might have supposed they would have thought of their danger. They didn't. I don't think anyone could have in their position.

For now they saw something not only behind the wave but behind the sun.

It was a range of mountains — high heights. Ever higher, ever higher, ever higher.

> ...any mountains even a quarter of a twentieth of that height ought to have had ice and snow on them. But these were warm and green and full of forests and waterfalls however high you looked. And suddenly there came a breeze from the east, tossing the top of the wave into foamy shapes and ruffling the smooth water all round them. It lasted only a second or so but what it brought them in that second none of those three children will ever forget. It brought both a smell and a sound, a musical sound...Lucy [said], 'It would break your heart.'

Exquisite to the point of pain. Have you been there in Christ? Are you there? His beauty is so exquisite it is painful: Christ.

That moment is where I go on alone. Child of God, there are only so many of us going on alone. One out of a company, one out of a family, one out of a church — alone. That's how few really want to go, how few have seen and known and been entranced with the beauty of holiness, the beauty of holiness.

> For one split second they saw [Reepicheep in his coracle]. Then it vanished, and since that moment no one can truly claim to have seen [him again]. But my belief is that he came safe to Aslan's country

— that is, to God —

> and is alive there to this day...
> ...But between them and the foot of the sky

— you see, they were at the horizon —

> there was something so white on the green grass that even

with their eagles' eyes they could hardly look at it. They came on and saw that it was a Lamb.

'Come and have breakfast,' said the Lamb in its sweet milky voice.

Then they noticed for the first time that there was a fire lit on the grass and fish roasting on it. They sat down and ate the fish, hungry now for the first time for many days. And it was the most delicious food they had ever tasted.

Food prepared by Christ. They had crossed the horizon. Oh, child of God. Food prepared by Christ!

'Please, Lamb,' said Lucy, 'is this the way to Aslan's country?'

Is this the way to God's abiding place?

'Is there a way into Aslan's country from our world too?'

'There is a way into my country from all the worlds,' said the Lamb; but as he spoke his snowy white flushed into tawny gold and his size changed and he was Aslan himself...

The Lion, the Christ, the Lamb of God, the Lion of the Tribe of Judah — He is waiting for us, at the horizon. He is waiting for us: the Lamb through whose blood we may cross becomes the Lion of the Tribe of Judah, taking us into the dwelling place of God.

'Oh, Aslan,' said Lucy, 'will you tell us how to get into your country from our world?'

'I shall be telling you all the time...'

That is what God is doing today. Via the blood of the Lamb, by the power of the Lion of Judah, to God's country.

And there shall be stability in thy times, abundance of

salvation, wisdom and knowledge: the fear of the Lord is his treasure (Is 33:6).

He shall dwell on high: his place of defence shall be the munitions of rocks: his bread shall be given him; his waters shall be sure. Thine eyes shall see the king in his beauty (vv. 16–17).

That's what lies beyond the horizon. We may cross that horizon (some of us have crossed it) here and now in this life and dwell where He dwells, in God's country. We come by the Lamb into the strength of God. This morning as Mr Black was using a part of Scripture the words came, 'Strength and Beauty'. Strength and Beauty: they are synonymous in God.

Thine eyes shall see the king in his beauty: they shall behold a land of far distances (v. 17: margin).

He will put us into 'a large place'. How large? The dwelling place of God, a land without horizons, a land of far distances. Glory to His name! It's for those who are washed and made pure in the blood of the Lamb, for those whose strength is the Lion, Christ Jesus. Why is it not for all of us? It is our choice.

Look upon Zion, the city of our solemnities: thine eyes shall see Jerusalem a quiet habitation, a tent that shall not be removed, the stakes whereof shall never be plucked up, neither shall any of the cords thereof be broken (v. 20).

This has God provided. This is yours, this is mine, for the taking. We only take what we want, don't we? We refuse what we don't want. That's what each one of us is doing right now. We are taking or refusing.

But there the Lord will be with us in majesty, a place of broad rivers and streams; wherein shall go no galley with oars, neither shall gallant ship pass thereby (v. 21).

There will be no commerce there. There will be nothing of man there. It is God's, that broad river is God's — God's love, God's power.

> And the inhabitant shall not say, I am sick: the people that dwell therein shall be forgiven their iniquity (v. 24).

You see, there cannot be iniquity in that place; 'Touch not the unclean thing.' Do you see the King in His beauty? Not twenty, thirty, forty years ago, according to your age, but now? Be ye spiritual, *now*. No scent, no sound from the forests round about will tempt us to take one day, one hour, one moment outwith the clear path where our eyes are always beholding the horizon.

Appeal

Will you cross over? God is here to take you. Whiteness of Christ, fragrance of lilies, purity, the light of the glory of the Godhead. The Lamb and the Lion: they are here, they are here. O God! What Thou hast prepared for those who love Thee — who *love* Thee. How near are you, child of God? Is the fragrance of the lily rich in your nostrils? Have your eyes been strengthened, and strengthened, and strengthened, that you can behold that glory, that shining, that light? Are you crying out, 'I can't bear any more, but don't let it stop. Strengthen me, Lord. Let me go nearer, and bear it.' It is not a dream, it is not a mirage. This is reality. Oh, be not besmirched. Don't allow sin to touch you: you belong to Christ. You belong to Christ! You are part of Him, part of the body. Don't let sin touch you, not for a moment. Touch not the unclean thing — neither in thought nor in word nor in action, within or outwith yourself. He is jealous, jealous. Not condemnation unto death, but unto life. Restored horizon. Stability shall be yours. 'There shall be stability in thy times.' No more seeking satisfaction other than in Christ. Abundance of salvation, abundance of the life of Christ. A love for holiness, which is a love for God. O Rabboni, Rabboni!

Across the horizon, O God! Across into that which is beyond, in time, O Lord, I come, I come. Take these tawdry things, these tawdry things, O God, take them. They are hindering, they are blocking my vision. They prevent my seeing clearly that which is mine in Thyself. They prevent me desiring passionately to please Thee, O Lord God of Hosts.

PROPHECY: This have I prepared in love for thee. For this did I create thee, that thou wouldst journey towards Me, that thou wouldst become holiness unto thy Lord, that earth and heaven would meet and merge and thou shouldst pass through, while yet in time; thou shouldst have a foretaste of that which is laid up for thee in eternity. I come that I might readjust thy walk. I come that I might strip thee of the weights that are heavy upon thee, that hinder thee. I come that thou mightest seek a purging from thy sin, cleansing from thy waywardness, from thy determination to have thine own way. I come; I will receive thee — but not with thy sin, not with thy folly. Thou must needs come again to Calvary. Thou must needs come again to that place in reality where thou canst be cleansed, where thou canst start afresh, where I may wash thine eyes with eye salve, that I might show thee again the horizon, that thou wouldst journey forward, not satisfied alone to reach the horizon, but with an overwhelming, surging love and desire to go beyond. I am come, My children, I am come with pleading, I am come with love, for I would have you spotless, without blemish, without wrinkle, or any such thing. I am preparing you for My Son. The day is far spent; the night is at hand; and the dawn shall be the dawn of the eternal day: the coming of the Bridegroom.

My son, give Me thy heart. My child, give Me thy heart.

PRAYER: God our Father, we would ask that not one shall retain their independence from Thee, but that each one shall choose Thy way, and shall put away from their thinking their own way, that they shall put on the garment which Thou hast designed, which Thou hast provided, that we all might remain in that wedding feast in that day, that none shall be turned away. Lord, we thank Thee for Thy patience, we thank Thee for Thy oft-speaking, we thank Thee for Thy love. In Christ's name, Amen.

Note

[1] C. S. Lewis, *The Voyage of the Dawn Treader* (Geoffrey Bles, 1952; Fontana Lions ed., 1980). Excerpts are taken from the last chapter.

IV

HOME CALL

1

AND THE TRUMPETS SOUNDED

[Miss Taylor died on 25 April 1991, and her funeral service took place in Struthers Memorial Church, Greenock on 29 April. Since this may be of interest to a wide circle, part of the service is included here. Unless otherwise indicated, the speaker's voice is my own.]

PRAYER: Lord our God, we are conscious of Thine own presence, of the brooding of the Holy Spirit upon us as we wait before Thee today. And, O God, we would be unhurried in Thy presence, with an ear that is open to Thy word, with an eye that is open to the Lord Jesus Christ. For, O God, there is so often a great mistake in gatherings such as these. It is very natural for the focus of attention to be on the departed, and there is a time and a place for that. But, O God, above and beyond and over all, there is the consciousness of God, the consciousness of Christ, and we pray that we shall have things in a true focus, that Thine shall be the glory, and ours shall be the blessing. We ask it in His name and for His sake. Amen.

A Unique Occasion

This funeral service will be different from any I have ever taken, and it may be different from any I will ever take again. So do not expect just the readings that are normally given and the lines that are normally followed.

For many a day, many a year indeed, I used to think, 'The day may come when I'll have this service to take,' and I was not at all sure that I would easily be able to do it. You don't work with someone as I worked with Miss

Taylor for, I suppose, between forty and fifty years, without feeling. And I knew of the danger of the emotional side. But a very wonderful thing happened, and I would like it to happen for all of you. I was with Miss Taylor an hour or thereabouts before she passed over, and I knew the anointing of God and the power of God, and my spirit was happy in Christ in that hour. Alison and I left her, and Mary and Grace remained. Soon we had a phone call to say that she had passed. And as we were travelling back to the hospital, without any thought, without any preparation, without any psychological doing of anything, I can only say that the glory of God fell on me. I suddenly realized the livingness into which Miss Taylor had entered, the intensity of life and of power and of joy and of glory and of release, and it so came over my spirit that all thought of a tragic service passed away: for it is not night, it is morning over there. And I want to read you what was in *Streams of the Desert* for the day of her departure.

The Folly of Grief

And there was Mary Magdalene and the other Mary; sitting over against the sepulchre (Mt 27:61).

How strangely stupid is grief. It neither learns nor knows nor wishes to learn or know. When the sorrowing sisters sat over against the door of God's sepulchre, did they see the two thousand years that have passed triumphing away? Did they see anything but this: 'Our Christ is gone!'

Your Christ and my Christ came from their loss. Myriad mourning hearts have had resurrection in the midst of their grief; and yet the sorrowing watchers looked at the seed-form of this result, and saw nothing. What they regarded as the end of life was the very preparation for coronation; for Christ was silent that He might live again in tenfold power.[1]

That was the reading for the day of her triumph.

I am reminded of a time when there was someone who passed away, and there was gloom on the church, and she in the Spirit gripped it, broke the gloom, and under God brought the triumph. And it is our privilege to try to do the same for her today.

[There followed singing from the Greenock choir, as they stood around the coffin, and 'The Holy City' from Owen Martin.]

I think you may appreciate that Miss Taylor would very deeply have appreciated this arrangement — she always wanted to be buried from the church, and I think she would have been delighted to be surrounded by her choir.

Angelic Presence

There is an interval of time between the spirit's being released from the body and the moment of clinical death. In these few minutes, again and again the presence of God becomes intense. Angelic presence sometimes fills the room, and those who experience that are peculiarly blessed. And there were two who experienced it. I have asked them to come and to tell the company a little about it.

Grace Gault

When we received the message that Miss Taylor had deteriorated and we went to the hospital, she was unconscious. As I sat there by her bedside along with others, one part was in grief. I knew that there was no way I could have wished her back, because she was going into peace and into light. I picked up her Bible that was lying at her bedside and opened it to see if God would speak. And He did, almost immediately. It opened at a psalm, and my eye fell on a verse that I knew was very precious to her because it was the one that God gave her as her own mother was dying and she was alone with her. It was, 'He giveth to his beloved in sleep' (Ps 127:2 margin). And I felt that she would just sleep sweetly and deeply away into Christ.

But there was still laboured breathing every so often, and there was the feeling that that was interfering with her peace. But when Mr Black came and prayed there was a tremendous sense of going over, that she was going through the valley, and in some way we were being privileged with the consciousness of going through that valley with her. And I became aware, as I think I had never been before, that the last great enemy to be faced is death, and there is that river to be crossed. But for the soul that is in Christ there is no danger. The enemy cannot touch that soul. I had a sense of the valley filling with light, and that Christ was coming to meet her in that valley and would take His child home.

And after my father and Alison had gone Miss Taylor's body began to relax, and increasingly it was like a soul falling asleep. Our eyes were shut most of the time, and we were praying. I could almost see her with an inner seeing, just going into Christ. His word was being fulfilled: 'He giveth to His beloved in sleep.' And there came a point where I could see that she was in His arms, and I knew she had fallen asleep in Christ. I thought, 'She's gone; she must have gone.' I waited for the breathing to stop, because I knew she was there. And Christ's presence was so beautiful. It is indeed the Christ that we meet every day. It is the Christ that so many of us found directly or indirectly through her ministry. And there is a sense of Him caring for those of us left behind with grief in our hearts, and caring for the one who has gone into such light and into such blessing. Praise His lovely name!

He is our Christ, and He will not be a stranger to us; He will come just like that for each one of us who know Him. We are joined to Him. As Miss Taylor's spirit went further and further over that valley and into

Christ, I felt her growing nearer and nearer to my spirit; I felt her growing more and more vividly alive, and as though our spirits were nearer than they had ever been. Blessed be Christ. We sorrow not as those without hope: we shall see those that we love again alive in Christ Jesus.

Mary Black

[Only fragments of Mary's contribution are included here since it appears in another form in the next chapter.]

The piece that Owen sang is one that was very precious to Miss Taylor. I took her a tape one night of his singing of it, and she was very deeply moved, especially when it came to the line, 'And the shadow of a cross arose upon a lonely hill.' There was a sense too, over recent weeks, of her spirit very deeply hankering after that New Jerusalem: to be gone from this earth scene and into the glory of God. Latterly her body was subject to more and more pain and discomfort, and there was a cry for the glory, for the eternal scene.

. . . . .

About half an hour after Miss Taylor died we went back into the room and I was astonished at the glory that had come in during that succeeding half hour. It was like walking into a sheet of light. The air was throbbing with the presence of the glory of God. And there is one thing of which I am absolutely sure. She is happy. She is in the glory. Her spirit is free at last. I had a sense also that Satan could not get at her any more through her body or through her mind, through anything at all. She is absolutely certainly in the glory of the presence of our Lord, and we shall meet her there in the glory. Praise His Name.

Mr Black Resumes

There is a custom in England which is not so prevalent in Scotland, the system of godfathers and godchildren. So far as I am aware, Miss Taylor had only one godchild; he was a godson. That godson has found Christ and is deeply moving with Him these days. And Andrew has been asked to sing what is a totally new song (words and music) on this occasion: 'Lay Your Life Gently'.

> Lay your life gently,
> Lay your life gently
> Down at the cross,
> Lay your life gently,
> Lay your life gently,
> Lay it right down at the cross.
>
> Lead my soul gently
> In the morning of life,
> Lead my soul gently on,
> Lead my soul gently
> In the noontime of life,
> Gentle the rays of the sun.
>
> Lead my soul gently
> In the twilight of life,
> Gentle the evening stars come,
> Lead me on gently
> Till the last goodnight
> Calls my soul gently home,
> Calls my soul gently home.

A Wise Builder

The first reading is from the writings of Paul:

> According to the grace of God which was given unto me, as a wise master builder I laid a foundation; and another buildeth thereon. But let each man take heed how he buildeth thereon. For other foundation can no man lay than that which is laid, which is Jesus Christ. But if any man buildeth on the foundation gold, silver, costly stones, wood, hay, stubble; each man's work shall be made manifest: for the day shall declare it, because it is revealed in fire; and the fire itself shall prove each man's work of what sort it is. If any man's work shall abide which he built thereon, he shall receive a reward. If any man's work shall be burned, he shall suffer loss: but he himself shall be saved; yet as through fire (1 Cor 3:10–15).

Resurrection

And secondly, from the story of Lazarus, who has died:

> So when Jesus came, he found that he had been in the tomb four days already (Jn 11:17).

I am sure that most of you are familiar with the story of Mary and Martha, the sorrowing company, the weeping Christ, and then the miracle of resurrection.

> Jesus saith unto her, Thy brother shall rise again. Martha saith unto him, I know that he shall rise again in the resurrection at the last day. Jesus said unto her, I am the resurrection and the life: he that believeth on me, though he die, yet shall he live: and whosoever liveth and believeth on me shall never die. Believest thou this? She saith unto him, Yea, Lord: I have believed that thou art the Christ, the Son of God, even he that cometh into the world (Jn 11:23–7).

And then we come further. We find that Christ Himself weeps at their unbelief, and He speaks that wonderful word: Lazarus comes forth, and mourning is turned to wonderful joy.

Recollections

You will appreciate that for me it is unusually difficult to be selective in my comments today. There were so many happenings of tremendous note over that long period of years, most of half a century. But I mean to touch one or two points that were particularly significant.

From a background where God was honoured Miss Taylor became an atheist because of the suffering that came into the family with the death of her father, leaving a very young family behind. Her deceased brother George was responsible for her going to hear Principal George Jeffreys in Greenock Town Hall in 1929. With a hard, hard heart she went, not with any interest in the meetings but just to accompany her widowed mother. There came a night when for some reason her mother could not go, and almost against her own will, without understanding why, she found herself there. And she found in that meeting that the living God spoke to her. For years she did not remember who the preacher was; he was so hidden behind the cross. But there came on her fearful conviction of sin: the sin of denying God. She went home to her own room and she told me, 'The carpet was like a pool of tears. I knew the wrath of an offended God, whose existence I had denied, whom I knew then with an absolute knowledge lived.' She went through a fearful time. Then suddenly there came a gentler light. In the mid-distance she saw the Lord Jesus Christ. He touched her, and she was made perfectly whole. The burden of her sin rolled away, and she rose to serve the living God.

That was many years ago, in 1929. Her brother George has gone, and his wife. Bertie, another brother, has gone, with Addis, whom you knew. And there now remains of that family Donald, who is a little older than herself, and his wife Cathie.

A FIRST MEETING: The years passed, and it was quite a number of years after that when I first met her: probably about sixteen years. And you know, I'll never forget when that happened. I was in a service, sitting in front of where she was. And I heard a voice, and I listened to a prayer, and I realized that there was a relationship with Christ of which I had no knowledge.

I was saved, all right; I was baptized in the Holy Spirit — but in listening to that one prayer, the tone of the voice, the expression, the language, I knew I had found someone who loved Christ. I think for the first time in my life I found someone who loved Christ passionately. And the number of people whom I know who really love Christ passionately I could count, I think, on my fingers. She loved him with an intensity that was transmitted to me. I made a point of finding her, and I learned from her. Like so many of you who are gathered here today, I sat at her feet and learned spiritual wisdom.

THE IMPARTING OF GIFT: I suppose that when I first received the gift of tongues as distinct from utterance at the time of the baptism it was through her ministry. She encouraged me into prophecy. Never shall I forget the night in the late Miss McKellar's house when in a prayer group there fell a mantle upon me from heaven, and I found that God was there and He commissioned me in a particular way and gave me what He has never taken away through all the years. That came through personal prophecy. She was deeply gifted and anointed of God.

You will realize that time fails me to speak of the numbers who came into the baptism through her ministry, the many who were delivered from demon power. But there was one ministry which I think delighted her above all other ministries in which she was used. It may have been the deepest of all, and it is perhaps the rarest of all. In our own midst there are one or two, but very few, who exercise it. It is very unsensational, it is very unseen. It is the ministry whereby she was able to take people into a particular love relationship with Christ. Something happened in lives in whom that miracle took place, and they were never the same again, changed at such deep levels.

AN EARLY VISION: I skip back just for a moment. I have got to a time in life when I sometimes repeat stories. If they are good stories they bear repeating, and in any case audiences change. But, you know, there is one story that I don't remember ever mentioning publicly. I have often told of the vision of the getting of this church, which I had on the hillside many years before it materialized. I seldom if ever have spoken of another experience from that same hillside. It happened in my very early days in Pentecost. I was alone on the hillside, looking at Greenock cemetery in the distance, and it was as though a communication or a thought went right through my mind that I have remembered through all the decades: *Myriads shall rise to call her blessed* (cf. Pro 31:28). And indeed from that cemetery and from cemeteries around the country, there are many who in the day of the Lord will rise to call her blessed. Blessed be His name.

THE POWER OF BINDING AND LOOSING: There were other sides to her ministry. She had the power of binding and loosing (Mt 18:18). There are two young men sitting in the church today (by a strange coincidence they are sitting within feet of each other) who were both very deeply backslidden, and there was no indication in the life of either that they would ever return to Christ. She told me one day, 'God has spoken to me about these two. They will both come back to Christ.' It seems that

147

in Christ she had the power to go into that spiritual world and set them free. And what was more awful, when the church was being troubled I have known her bind an enemy. She fought for the church of God: the power of binding and loosing. A little, frail lady, in whom the power of the living God throbbed.

VISION OF CHURCHES: I come to vision. She had many. She fought Satan in her own room until she had a backbone like steel, and when she came out into the field of deliverance she was iron-firm and demons fled. Men and women went prostrate under the power of God in her ministry. But on the vision side, there is one I felt particularly to bring before you today. It came on the last day of a camp. She went into the Spirit, and she was out of the body. I was with her when she came back into consciousness, and she told me the promise that God gave her. She saw the church here. She saw the churches left and right extending, and she received the promise of God that they would continue until Christ Himself returned. So I have always known since then that no matter what storm rises, what waves break, the work will go on: it is the promise of the living God. 'The gates of hell shall not prevail against it.' No man, no woman, will ever destroy that which is under the sealed promise of God.

'I laid a foundation,' Paul said. 'For other foundation can no man lay than that which is laid, which is Jesus Christ.' She built on the sure foundation of Christ.

A FAITHFUL BUILDER: Time does not permit me to go in detail into the construction of buildings. But there are many of you here who know that the builder builds with a plumb line, up and down and across. Miss Taylor built on Christ, and she was a faithful builder. She had a vision, she had a commission, and she would not alter the plan by a hairbreadth. There were many over the years who did try to alter it — take it this way, take it that way, take it the other way. She would have none of it. She would be rid of them before she would deviate. And this is a continual temptation in the work of God: to smooth it, water it down, make things easier, more reasonable, more accommodating. Very recently I saw a little bridge. It was a beautiful bridge, and at a distance it could have been a very admirable bridge. But as I got nearer, I saw it was made of wood. Beautiful, but made of wood. And in an hour of fire it would burn up. There are today many beautiful 'works of God' that will burn to the last cinder in the hour of God's testing, because they are not solid on the rock Christ Jesus. They are of wood. She built gold, silver, and precious stones.

Abundant Harvest

And, oh, I rejoice in my spirit. I am getting on, as you well know, and for a short moment when I sensed the release into which she had gone, I too knew what it would be like to carry no responsibility, to go home. I don't think my going is imminent, but I can understand what it feels like: the blessedness of going into the presence of God. But surely none of us wants to go in there before the work is done — before the work is done. There was one area in which she longed for fruit over the years. And while there was fruit, maybe more abundant fruit than in many places, it was not so abundant as in some other areas of her ministry. It was healing. I don't know whether God has given a special departing present, but I would say that the last three years may have been the most fruitful this movement has ever known. Last weekend between fifty-five and seventy people came for ministry where some of us were. I have known a hundred per cent of a company come for ministry. But what has been remarkable is the increase in healings: sometimes instantaneous healings. One last Monday, one a week or two before it, and one within the last sixteen hours: instantaneous healing — sometimes just where the congregation sit, as they gather, knowing the presence of God. It is as though He has taken His servant home and her works do follow her. The gifts that came into operation so often under her ministry are in full flood, and there are more dedicated people in the midst of this church now than I have ever known in fifty years: many, many truly dedicated, straight up and down, according to the plumbline of God. I rejoice in my spirit today for her. Her works do follow her. And she rejoices today in the glory of God.

Deep Peace

I will have to miss certain things I wanted to say. But we will have the Glasgow choir sing 'Deep Peace', and then we will close with 'Ye gates, lift up your heads on high' — so often her own choice of a closing hymn for our conferences.

> Deep peace of the running wave to you,
> Deep peace of the flowing air to you,
> Deep peace of the quiet earth to you,
> Deep peace of the shining stars to you,
> Deep peace of the Son of Peace to you.

BENEDICTION: Now may the blessing of God rest and abide, for Christ's sake. Amen.

Note

[1] Mrs Charles H. Cowman, *Streams in the Desert* vol. 1 (Marshall Pickering, 1949; © 1949 and 1990, Cowman Publications), reading for 25 April.

2
LILAC TIME

Mary Black, Sheila Robertson and Ivy Anslow
speak of events around Miss Taylor's passing

[After a considerable time lapse, an article was prepared for the church magazine about Miss Taylor's
passing. The contributions carry their own flavour and
sweetness.]

Mary Black: 'The Watchers'

The room was warm and still. At the left hand side of
the bed two of us sat, heads bowed, eyes shut as quietness filled the air.

The harsh laboured breathing ceased; Miss Taylor's
face grew restful; the colour faded to pinched white as
her breathing became softer and softer. Then softer than
breath came the knowledge to the hearts of the
watchers her moment had come. The footfall of Christ
was at the bedside and He took His child in His arms. I
will never forget the sweetness of that moment, as her
soul passed out of time, not into a strange unknown but
into the arms of the Christ she knew so well, into that
warm, loving Presence she was so often used to convey
to those of us who sat under her ministry.

Oh, that dear familiar Presence — surely when we
see Him He will not be a stranger.

The words came to mind as that moment of meeting
between time and Eternity took place:

He giveth His beloved sleep (Ps 127:2 AV).

Her going was as simple and sweet as a child falling blissfully into sleep.

Time passed and still the watchers sat, and as they sat, there stole upon them the knowledge that others too were there. Heavenly watchers had waited for this moment, and now, as a soul passed further and further into the glory, the joy of those watching in Heaven could not be contained — and it spilled over Heaven's edges into our hearts, and so we too rejoiced.

NEW DAWN MAGAZINE: The glory that marked the moment of Miss Taylor's passing pervaded the atmosphere at the funeral also, and poured into the hearts of many as they met together in different locations over that weekend.

The words of T.S. Eliot, quoted by one of those who felt the glory of that time, sum up for us the sense of Resurrection which came to our hearts:

> April is the cruellest month, breeding
> Lilacs out of the dead land, mixing
> Memory and desire, stirring
> Dull roots with spring rain.[a]

We truly felt that spring rain stir us to the roots of our being, refreshing our heart's endeavour to follow hard after the Christ she knew and loved so well.

The weekend immediately following her passing was accompanied by a peculiar sense of God's rich and vital presence in the midst of us. Perhaps we were allowed an overflow of the joy which that moment of being united perfectly to Christ must have brought to her.

---

[a] From 'The Waste Land'. For the interpretation of these lines, see Sheila's contribution below.

Sheila Robertson: 'A Time for Lilacs'

On the Saturday evening between Miss Taylor's death and her funeral, we held our normal prayer meeting at six o'clock in the church. I was aware from the outset that the presence of God was strangely near — there was such a rich overshadowing of His love for His children.

As we were praying, a picture began to emerge in my mind. I saw a coffin being lowered into a grave. There was no human hand near the coffin — it was not being held up by ropes; rather, it seemed suspended in mid-air, in its final lowering into the earth.

The most remarkable sight drew my attention — the lid of the coffin was strewn with lilacs. It was absolutely covered in them, both white and purple lilacs — an utter abundance of them. This was no formal floral tribute, nor yet a small token of remembrance — this was an overwhelming shower of beautiful blossoms, in the fullness of bloom as if someone had taken armfuls of flowers and thrown them on the descending coffin — an overabundance of thought and love being sent with the blooms.

Dylan Thomas speaks in 'Poem in October' of going for a walk on his thirtieth birthday, in 'a shower of all my days'.

It was as if the lilacs represented a 'shower' of all her days — the abundant life which had come from her life and the abundant life which was yet to come in the church, because of her example and ministry.

However, on the Saturday evening I had only the vague imprint on my mind — and no thought of what it all meant. In fact I would never have mentioned it to anyone, had a friend in the church not given me a birthday card at the end of the prayer time. I opened it — and on it was a picture of lilacs in a vase!!!

In my awe and consternation, I blurted out, *'Elaine, I've just seen LILACS all over Miss Taylor's coffin! Can you believe it?'*

Good friend that she is, she nodded and confided in

me that she had in fact been drawn to that card and had chosen it with special care. Little did she know when she bought it, that it was the spur that was necessary for me to speak of what I had seen.

I was still puzzled the next day (Sunday) as to what it had all meant. I was sure God had spoken, and the confirmation came in Elaine giving me the card — yet what was the significance to me and to the church?

Still pondering these thoughts in my mind, I was sitting upstairs near the phone, when I caught sight of a book in the bookshelf. It was *Selected Poems* of T.S. Eliot and I decided to leaf through it. Had I been looking for poems or books to explain the meaning of lilacs (or even to throw some light on the subject) I would have chosen Wordsworth or Keats, yet I felt to read T.S. Eliot! What would a modernist (an unromantic American) have to say about lilacs? All I could remember from my studies of the poet in university days was his 'burnt-out ends of smoky days' — an image of dissolute living.

I also remembered that Prufrock had said in 'The Lovesong of J. Alfred Prufrock', 'I have measured out my life with coffee spoons' — a bit like myself in the old days but not a lifestyle to be imitated!

What light could T.S. Eliot throw on my dilemma? Yet, there was the answer underneath my fingertips. I flipped over from 'Prufrock', past 'Gerontion', past 'Burbank with a Baedeker' to 'THE WASTE LAND' (1922), which opened with the following:

1 *The Burial of the Dead*

> April is the cruellest month, breeding
> Lilacs out of the dead land, mixing
> Memory and desire, stirring
> Dull roots with spring rain.

I couldn't believe my eyes! In the margin I had written, 'It brings regeneration' — new life! I had used the book nineteen years previously when I'd been at university and now the poem and the notes were being used to speak to me in 1991!

God was indicating to me that new life was going to spring from death — manifold life from one death. Death was not the end but a new dawn. This applied to the life of our church — from Miss Taylor's life, witness, ministry and death would come new life in Christ — a fresh impetus into the harvest field, new reapers who would work alongside the workers of many years to reap what they did not sow. We would be the beneficiaries of a legacy of a life laid down on the altar for Christ.

We are reminded of the New Year word (from two or three years ago), 'The latter glory of this house shall be greater than that of the former.' What an inheritance we have in Christ Jesus!

Not long after I had spoken in the church of what I had seen in April, a letter arrived for me from Swansea, from Miss Ivy Anslow, containing news of a most amazing occurrence. With her permission, I record here the contents of part of that letter:

> I was very interested when listening to a tape dated 4 May 1991 to hear of your experience following the passing away of Miss Taylor that the vision of lilacs covering her coffin brought to you some precious truth. As I listened, I was filled with awe, because I had an identical experience and felt I should share it with you.
>
> When Mr Black phoned me to tell me Miss Taylor had passed over, there was a great sense of loss, but also an awareness of her new state and glorious liberation from earthly bonds ...
>
> For two weeks after Miss Taylor's funeral I felt a desire to spend time in my bedroom during the evening to listen to the tapes rather than remain in the lounge. I sat in my armchair near the large window which overlooks the neighbour's garden and I gazed in wonder upon a very large white lilac tree, which in ten years had never blossomed like that. Its branches were heavy with thick

white blooms just in front of my wall. It brought with it such sheer delight, I can only say I was blessed. There was something so special about it, I kept remarking on it.

One evening, as I was looking at it, I felt the drawing near of Christ. There was an awesomeness in His presence and the atmosphere was otherworldly. I felt God was speaking and when I heard you speak on the tape regarding your own searching for and finding of the meaning of the lilac (regeneration) it was so significant — for there is a reproducing of the same life in the church.

Out of the mouths of two witnesses! — hundreds of miles apart (one in Scotland, one in Wales) a similar revelation is given! Praise be to God — His ways are not hidden from us. He makes His meaning clear to us, that we might not be mistaken in the path He has made for us.

NOTE TO READERS

If you would like to enquire further about issues raised in this book or if you feel that the compiler could be of help, you are invited to write to him at 27 Denholm Street, Greenock, PA16 8RH, Scotland, or telephone 0475 787432.

It may also be of interest to know that Hugh Black is normally involved in five conferences in Scotland each year — New Year, Easter, July, August and October. Friends gather from many parts of Britain. An open invitation is extended to all and particularly to those interested in the baptism in the Holy Spirit and related themes. Details will be provided on enquiry.

NEW DAWN BOOKS BY HUGH BLACK

Reflections on the Baptism in the Holy Spirit *£2.25* This book is already proving very popular and is being used in bringing people into the baptism in the Spirit. It has been described as one of the clearest, most incisive books on this subject.

Reflections on the Gifts of the Spirit *£2.75* Deals in an original way with its subject. The chapters on miracles, healings and discernment (with exorcism) have roused great interest and led to positive action. Anecdotes and illustrations have been much appreciated.

Reflections on a Song of Love *£1.25* A highly original commentary on 1 Cor 13. The drawing power of love pervades this fascinating study. The author shows very clearly how this chapter fully supports and in no way detracts from the doctrine of Pentecost.

A Trumpet Call to Women *£2.50* Presents a strong case from Scripture for greater involvement of women in ministry. It throws much light on those portions which on the surface seem to put women in a subject role. It includes the testimony of Elizabeth H. Taylor, a lady much used of God. A stirring book, demanding a response — a call to action.

Consider Him *£2.25* Considers a number of the qualities of Christ. He Himself seems to speak from the pages of the book, both in the main text and in the testimony of Jennifer Jack, whose selfless presentation truly leaves the reader to consider Christ.

Battle for the Body *£2.95* It will take courage to face the truths highlighted in this original approach to fundamental issues of sanctification. The second part presents the powerful testimony of John Hamilton — a preacher widely known and loved.

The Clash of Tongues: With Glimpses of Revival *£2.75* Part One is a commentary on 1 Cor 14. It deals in detail with some of the more difficult questions. Part Two deals with the relationship between revival and Pentecost and refers to the 1939 and 1949 revivals in Lewis, introducing a number of participants in the former — particularly Mary MacLean, whose remarkable testimony is related. This book will particularly appeal to the studiously inclined.

The Incomparable Christ *£2.75* Part One deals with the gospel. It faces honestly the questions of Christ's resurrection and that of all men. It deals in a direct way with the doctrine of hell and eternal judgment, and gives practical instruction on the way of salvation. Part Two presents the remarkable testimonies of two young ladies.

Gospel Vignettes *£2.95* Focuses attention on various facets of the gospel, such as The Life-Giving Water, Weighed in the Balances. Includes testimonies of three people whose lives have been transformed by Christ, to one of whom Christ Himself appeared. Useful in the gospel, but introducing the pentecostal dimension.

Reflections from Abraham *£2.50* Outlines spiritual principles seen in the life of Abraham. It deals with his call and ours, the mountain as distinct from the valley life, intercession, Lot in Sodom, the sacrifice of Isaac and the way of faith. Part Two tells of the action of God in the life of Dorothy Jennings.

Reflections from Moses: With the Testimony of Dan McVicar *£2.99*
Part One shows the outworking of spiritual principles such as the calling and training of a man of God, the need to start from holy ground, deliverance from bondage, and the consequences of Moses' failure in a critical hour. Part Two presents the well-known evangelist Dan McVicar's story in his own words. The conversion of this militant communist and the intervention of God in the lives of his parents make thrilling reading.

Christ the Deliverer *£2.99* Deals with both physical and spiritual deliverance. It includes a number of remarkable testimonies to healing, e.g. from blindness, manic depression, ME, rheumatoid arthritis, spinal injury, phobias, nightmares. It speaks of the appearance of angels, touches on revival and analyses the theory of 'visualization'.

Christian Fundamentals *£3.50* Part One deals with the individual and his needs in the realms of Salvation, Baptism in the Spirit, and Deliverance. Part Two focuses on the outflow of the life of God to meet the needs of others through Vocal,

Hidden and Open Power Ministries. The End Times are the subject of Part Three.

Reflections from David £3.75 This searching book shows a man after God's own heart in the glory of his achievements and the tragedy of his failings. Divine retribution and forgiveness, the joy of deliverance, and the action of God in present-day lives are all examined.

Pioneers of the Spiritual Way £4.99 From a lost Eden our race walked a lost road, occasionally experiencing higher things as pioneers of the spiritual way led upwards. The impassable barrier between God and man was finally removed as the last Adam blasted a way through: Christ, bringing many sons to glory.

Revival: Including the Prophetic Vision of Jean Darnall £3.99
Some great revivals of the past are reviewed with their enduring principles and changing patterns. Revival comes nearer as we are confronted with more recent movements of God. The celebrated vision of Jean Darnall has left many with a feeling of keen expectation for coming days.

Revival: Personal Encounters £4.50 From the treasure chest of memory the author brings a series of revival-related incidents, from Africa and Brazil to the island of Lewis and an unusual Scottish school camp. The highly original testimony of Alison Speirs brings the challenge of revival right to our doorstep. A dynamic book.

Revival: Living in the Realities £3.99 Describes how revival living is outworked. This book ponders issues such as spiritual warfare, what it means to be imitators of Christ, the need to progress from forgiveness to love for those who do us harm, and the mystery of the love of God itself. An unusual and thought-provoking approach.

BOOK ORDERS

The books advertised on the previous pages are being made available to Christian booksellers throughout the country, but if you have any difficulty in obtaining your supply, you may order directly from New Dawn Books, 10A Jamaica Street, Greenock, Renfrewshire, PA15 1YB.

·············· ORDER FORM ··············

Please send me the books indicated below:

Quantity	Title	Price
	Reflections on the Baptism in the Holy Spirit	£2.25
	Reflections on the Gifts of the Spirit	£2.75
	Reflections on a Song of Love (A commentary on 1 Cor 13)	£1.25
	A Trumpet Call to Women	£2.50
	Consider Him (Twelve Qualities of Christ)	£2.25
	Battle for the Body	£2.95
	The Clash of Tongues: With Glimpses of Revival	£2.75
	The Incomparable Christ	£2.75
	Gospel Vignettes	£2.95
	Reflections from Abraham	£2.50
	Reflections from Moses: With the Testimony of Dan McVicar	£2.99
	Christ the Deliverer	£2.99
	Christian Fundamentals	£3.50
	Reflections from David	£3.75
	Pioneers of the Spiritual Way	£4.99
	Revival: Including the Prophetic Vision of Jean Darnall	£3.99
	Revival: Personal Encounters	£4.50
	Revival: Living in the Realities	£3.99
	E. H. Taylor: A Modern Christian Mystic	£4.50

Signature ....

Address ....

....

....

When ordering please send purchase price plus 40p per book to help cover the cost of postage and packaging.